The Georgia Open History Library has been made possible in part by a major grant from the National Endowment for the Humanities: Democracy demands wisdom. Any views, findings, conclusions, or recommendations expressed in this collection, do not necessarily represent those of the National Endowment for the Humanities.

NATIONAL
ENDOWMENT
FOR THE
HUMANITIES

Frontispiece

[Description as recorded on the Peter Gordon Engraving.]

A View of Savanah as it stood the 29th of March, 1734. P. Gordon Inv. P. Fourdrinier Sculp. To the Honorable the Trustees for establishing the Colony of Georgia in America. This View of the Town of Savanah is humbly dedicated by the Honours Obliged and most Obedient Servant, Peter Gordon. Vüe de Savanah dans la Georgie.

1. The Stairs going up.
2. Mr. Oglethorpe's Tent.
3. The Crane & Bell.
4. The Tabernacle & Court House.
5. The Publick Mill.
6. The House for Strangers.
7. The Publick Oven.
8. The Draw Well.
9. The Lott for the Church.
10. The Publick Stores.
11. The Fort.
12. The Parsonage House.
13. The Pallisadoes.
14. The Guard House and Battery of Cannon.
15. Hutchinson's Island.

[The Size of the actual engraving: 15 7/8 by 21 3/4 inches.]

The Journal of
Peter Gordon
1732-1735

Edited by

E. MERTON COULTER

WORMSLOE FOUNDATION PUBLICATIONS
NUMBER SIX

UNIVERSITY OF GEORGIA PRESS

ATHENS

Copyright © 1963
UNIVERSITY OF GEORGIA PRESS

Library of Congress Catalog Card Number: 63-17348

Reissue published in 2021

Most University Press titles are available
from popular e-book vendors.

Printed digitally

ISBN 9780820359380 (Hardcover)
ISBN 9780820359373 (Paperback)
ISBN 9780820359366 (Ebook)

 *Contents*

FOREWORD TO THE REISSUE	vii
FOREWORD	xiii
INTRODUCTION	1
THE JOURNAL OF PETER GORDON, 1732–1735	23
NOTES	69
INDEX	75

Foreword To The Reissue

Peter Gordon's journal is significant to Georgia history not only because of its mere existence as one of the few eyewitness accounts of the colony's creation but also because of the many topics it addresses both directly and indirectly. Gordon (1699–1740) was one of the 114 passengers aboard the *Anne* that brought the first colonists to Georgia in February 1733 and therefore helped establish the new outpost.[1] Despite Georgia's relatively late founding in comparison with other mainland British colonies, it still faced similar challenging obstacles when it came to its construction. Gordon's commentary about those early days makes his journal an invaluable source for Georgia history.

His brief introduction to the larger narrative is often overlooked but should be viewed by scholars as a short yet important piece of promotional literature, which he fully intended his work to be upon publication. His overview of the Trustees' intentions and plans for their colony initially follows this same flattering portrayal of the prospects that existed in Georgia, but he quickly counters with criticisms of the Trustees' land policies regarding inheritance. This grievance about property distribution would become an important pillar in the campaign against the Trustees led by an opposition party that eventually became known as the Malcontents, but its appearance here in Gordon's work shows just how early that problem surfaced. It also reveals his political leanings, which emerge at various times throughout his narrative. His chronicle of the voyage to Georgia replicates the experiences of other immigrants and contributes to recent studies that look closely at the logistics of sea travel at this time.[2]

Most of Gordon's journal provides important details about exactly how those first colonists went about constructing the new outpost and conducting their daily lives. Studying social history has become standard operating procedure in academia; Gordon's work offers his own perspective on everyday life and allows scholars to compare and contrast his experiences with those of other colonial ventures in North America and around the world. It also offers many small accounts of individual experiences that may seem trivial to modern readers but that were obviously noteworthy enough at the time to deserve inclusion in his narrative. His remarks open up the opportunity for countless microhistories into the people who founded Georgia as well as give examples of the triumphs and tragedies that they faced during those early days.

Perhaps one of the most valuable aspects of Gordon's journal is his commentary about the Native peoples he encountered. It provides intriguing details about the first meetings between James Oglethorpe, the unofficial leader of the colony and the only Trustee ever to visit Georgia, and Tomochichi, the Yamacraw Creek headman whose people occupied the land Oglethorpe wanted to settle, and what occurred there. Gordon also witnessed several of the formal negotiations between these two men and gave detailed accounts of these early moments of British-Creek diplomacy. The significant role the Native peoples played in colonial and Georgia history remains an important and thriving avenue of research that has yet to be exhausted, and Gordon's account offers many lanes for future exploration.

Gordon did more than share his observations about the new world around him, however. He also stepped back to assess the situation in Savannah more broadly in terms of its progress as a town and as a community. He presented an overview of how the people transformed the landscape and created a viable city with basic amenities such as housing, roads, and public buildings. Perhaps more important, he examined the political situation in Savannah during those inaugural months and recognized that fissures were already starting to develop between the Trustees' dream of a well-regulated population that closely adhered to their vision for the colony and the residents' reality of a tropical environment inhabited by self-interested individuals who had their own agendas to fulfill. This disconnect between the overseas administrators and their colonial subjects would increase in the years to come, but Gordon's journal reveals that those problems began at the colony's inception.

Gordon was uniquely situated to comment on the political conditions in the colony because of his positions as a tythingman and as the first bailiff. Even though Gordon was classified as a "charity colonist" because the Trustees had paid for his passage to Georgia, they must have judged him to be trustworthy because they appointed him to these important offices. The tythingman oversaw the well-being of ten families during the passage to and on their arrival and settlement in the colony, and Oglethorpe chose four men to take on this task, including Gordon. The bailiff served as a justice of the colony, meaning that he acted as one of three judges that directed court sessions. In addition, the bailiffs nominally functioned as the leading officials of the colony because they held the highest appointed positions. Although they had no real power because the Trustees wanted to retain as much authority over their subjects as possible, the bailiffs still embodied the role of a colonial administrator unofficially.[3] Gordon's designation as first bailiff gave him no special standing or extra influence; it was simply the title that the Trustees used when they selected him for the post.[4] Besides the obvious yet unintended status that accompanied these positions, they also associated Gordon with the Trustees since they expected him to uphold and enforce their regulations.

Yet because Gordon disobeyed their commands—directly and indirectly—his writings are characterized by a certain anti-Trustee slant, which calls into question his dependability as an employee and as a historical source. Gordon eventually left the colony and returned to England without the Trustees' permission, which violated his terms of office, and he sympathized with the disgruntled residents who chafed under the Trustees' regulations by listening to and compiling their grievances to submit to the Trustees. Gordon explained some of those grievances toward the end of his journal, thus marking the start of many years of difficulties between the Trustees and their wayward colonists. Gordon's misbehavior on and off the job caused the Trustees to view him as insubordinate and therefore to dismiss any claims he brought to them in person regardless of their practicality.

Contributing to historians' suspicions about Gordon's integrity is his claim to the authorship of the famous engraving "A View of Savanah as it stood the 29th of March 1734." As George F. Jones has convincingly argued, Gordon did not pen this illustration, but he did take credit for it by signing, "Obliged and most Obedient Servant, Peter Gordon."[5] Why Gordon falsely asserted production of this document remains unknown, but this misrepresentation certainly taints his reputation among scholars.

Despite his questionable actions and intentions while in the colony, his opinions and observations remain invaluable to the study of early Georgia. Although dubbed a "journal" by E. Merton Coulter, who originally edited Gordon's manuscript, it reads more like a series of remarks and reflections about the world around him. Coulter concluded that Gordon must have assembled the final product upon his return to England but that he likely had kept some sort of records of his time in Georgia because of the detail he included. His writing style, however, lacks the specificity of precise and accurate dates as well as a more thorough accounting of all activities in the colony at that time.[6] Furthermore, it becomes more narrative and reflective over the course of the volume. This shift is especially apparent at the end when he presents an organized summary of the opposition's grievances.

Because of his appointed position as first bailiff, Gordon was especially attuned to the political situation in the new colony. Soon after mentioning the official establishment of the local government and court system, he shifted from a mere chronicler to an interested commentator about the situation around him. He opined about the proper role that the government should have in colonial oversight and criticized the arrangement that the Trustees had imposed on them as unwieldy and unworkable under the particular circumstances in the colony. He decried the Trustees' land and labor policies at length, and he condemned the partisanship and favoritism exhibited by certain local officials, such as Thomas Causton, a fellow bailiff. While Gordon's remarks mirror those arguments made by the Malcontents in later years, they represent the first time that these issues appeared and mark the beginning of the split into pro-Trustee and anti-Trustee factions. And although political history fell out of fashion in academia during the end of the twentieth century, it is witnessing a resurgence on all levels—local, state, and national. Revisiting the debates between the Trustees and the Malcontents in all their many iterations—especially these earliest ones—will contribute to the resurgence of this important field of study.

Thus, Gordon's journal continues to offer important insights into many aspects of early Georgia and to act as a valuable source of study for historians despite its obvious biases and unusual organization. Scholars, of course, know to examine all records with a degree of skepticism, and their approach to Gordon's narrative should be no different. Nevertheless, his commentary on the political, diplomatic, and social conditions during those early days provides important material from which historians can draw their own conclusions.

JULIE ANNE SWEET

Notes

1. This volume, 1; E. Merton Coulter and Albert B. Saye, eds., *A List of the Early Settlers of Georgia* (Athens: University of Georgia Press, 1949), 19.

2. Stephen R. Berry, *A Path in the Mighty Waters: Shipboard Life and Atlantic Crossings to the New World* (New Haven, Conn.: Yale University Press, 2015).

3. This volume, 1, 3–4; Kenneth Coleman, *Colonial Georgia* (New York: Charles Scribner's Sons, 1976), 91, 94–95.

4. *CRG*, 32: 12–13.

5. George F. Jones, "Peter Gordon's (?) Plan of Savannah," *Georgia Historical Quarterly* 70 (Spring 1986): 97–101. See also this volume, 6–8.

6. This volume, 18, 20.

 *Foreword*

THE Wormsloe Foundation is a non-profit organization chartered on December 18, 1951, by the Superior Court of Chatham County, Georgia. In the words of its charter, "The objects and purposes of this Foundation are the promotion of historical research and the publication of the results thereof; the restoration, preservation and maintenance of historical sites and documents and the conduct of an educational program in the study of history of the State of Georgia, and in states adjacent thereto."

As its first important activity, the Foundation has begun the publication of a series of historical works under the title of "Wormsloe Foundation Publications." They will consist of important manuscripts, reprints of rare publications, and historical narratives relating to Georgia and the South. The first volume appeared in 1955, written by E. Merton Coulter and entitled *Wormsloe: Two Centuries of a Georgia Family*. This volume gave the historical background of the Wormsloe estate and a history of the family which has owned it for more than two and a quarter centuries.

The second publication of the Foundation was *The Journal of William Stephens, 1741–1743* and the third volume was *The Journal of William Stephens, 1743-1745*, which is a continuation of the journal as far as any known copy of it is extant. However, it is known that Stephens kept up his journal for some years after 1745. Both of these volumes were edited by E. Merton Coulter and were published in 1958 and 1959, respectively. The fourth publication of the Foundation was the re-publication of the unique copy of Pat. Tailfer *et al., A True and Historical Narrative of the Colony of Georgia . . . With Comments by the Earl of Egmont,* in the John Carter Brown Library of Brown University. In this publication there appeared for the first time in print the comments of Egmont. With the permission of Brown University, this volume was edited by Clarence L. Ver Steeg.

The fifth volume in the series of Wormsloe Foundation Publications was the long-missing first part of Egmont's three manuscript volumes of his journal, edited by Robert G. McPherson. This volume contains the journal from 1732 to 1738, inclusive, and is owned by the Gilcrease Institute of American History and Art, who gave permission for its publication. The present volume is the journal of Peter Gordon, as is fully explained in the Introduction.

E. Merton Coulter
General Editor

Introduction

MOST people of America who have met Peter Gordon have run across him as the author or artist of a Plan or View or Design of Savannah; but recently a manuscript of his, which he calls a journal, has come to light and has been acquired by the University of Georgia Library.[1] It is here published for the first time.

Gordon must have been a man of some standing in England; his work as an upholsterer and his need for employment in 1732 recommended him to the favorable attention of the committee which had been appointed to select settlers for the Colony of Georgia, about to be founded south and west of the Savannah River. The Trustees in charge of the Colony made him an important official in the government to be set up there, and James Edward Oglethorpe, who was to be in immediate control of the Colony, seems at this time to have held Gordon in high esteem.

The ship *Ann* (also spelled *Anne*) sailed from England about the middle of November, 1732 (Old Style), with the first embarkation, which included Gordon, Oglethorpe, and 112 others—men, women, and children. On the voyage across the Atlantic, Oglethorpe informed Gordon that he had been appointed by the Trustees to be the first of four Tythingmen (Tithingmen), each of which was to be the head of ten families to see that they were properly provisioned and attended to on board the ship and afterward similarly looked after and protected in the Colony.

Less than a month out of Gravesend, whence they had sailed from England, Gordon became ill and continued so for the next dozen days, according to his account. Another on the voyage wrote that "Mr. Gordon was desparately ill of the Cholick."[2] He was at this time 34 (or 35) years old, and he was accompanied by his wife Catherine (also spelled Katherine), who was 28.[3]

When the ship reached Charles Town, South Carolina, according to Gordon, Oglethorpe asked him to put on his best dress and go on shore, there to convey to the Governor and Council Oglethorpe's compliments and to secure a pilot. Upon Gordon's suggesting that firing a gun was the customary way of securing a pilot, a gun was fired, but without effect, whereupon Oglethorpe was rowed ashore. The ship, with Oglethorpe back aboard, continued its trip on down the coast to Port Royal, where the colonists were to remain until Oglethorpe, assisted by some South Carolinians, should continue on to the Savannah River for the purpose of picking out a spot where the first settlement should be made.

Gordon states that on the voyage from Charles Town to Port Royal, a suspicious-looking vessel was spied, which had all the appearance of being a piratical craft, and that preparations were made to beat it off with gun fire; but the craft, on seeing these preparations, veered away. Gordon pays a special compliment to the women on board, who were anxious not only to hand up guns and ammunition but also to man the guns on top deck if needed. It is rather remarkable that no one else who has been found to have made this voyage and written about it, mentions any such an event.[4] However, the incident should not be considered a fabrication of Gordon's. It may be that he was a little overwrought by a return of his "Cholick," though he makes no mention of it.

INTRODUCTION　　　　　　　　　　　　　　　3

The colonists arrived at Yamacraw Bluff on February 1, 1732 (Old Style), or February 12, 1733 (New Style), and it should be noted here that all dates in the Gordon manuscript, as indeed in all English correspondence before 1752, are in Old Style. It was not until 1752 that, according to an enactment of the British Parliament, the New Style calendar was adopted, which provided that the next day following September 2nd should be September 14th; thus eleven days were dropped, and the new year began on January 1st instead of March 25th, as had been the custom theretofore.

This New Style calendar now made February 1st the 12th, and all Old Style dates were similarly affected. February 1st was now to be celebrated by these new arrivals as "Georgia Day," but after the change in the calendar, Georgia's birthday became the 12th, and was thereafter celebrated on that day. All dates between January 1st and March 25th prior to 1752 were advanced a year, and no longer hereafter during this period were the English people to write the year in the double notation, as February 1, 1732/33, in recognition of the change for the beginning date of the year, which had been in existence for centuries in some other parts of the world. Thus, Georgia was founded February 1, 1732, Old Style; but in the New Style it was February 12, 1733.

The colonists began immediately to clear the land by cutting the great wealth of pine trees, sawing and splitting them into clapboards, and constructing houses. Either because Oglethorpe liked to exercise authority or because he considered the people too busy developing their town and fields to be bothered by the erection of civil government, he made no move in this direction until July 7th, when the first court was held. Gordon occupied the place of honor as the First Bailiff [5] or Magistrate; there were three in all. The Bailiffs were the supreme authority in the local government, with the Recorder to keep the records, and with Constables, Tythingmen, and Conservators of the Peace to assist in preserving order and punishing evil-doers. In addition to being First Bailiff, Gordon was a Tythingman, and also a Conservator of the Peace. When not holding court he could act in these other capacities, but in fact he seemed to have worked in none appreciably. In the court held on July 28th he was absent,[6] and it is doubtful that he attended many sessions.

The first year in Georgia was a deadly one. No fewer than twenty-six of the settlers died that year, July being especially a devastating time. The first person to die was Dr. William Cox, the surgeon. His death was a bad loss, but Noble Jones stepped in to help when not busied with official duties. Gordon became ill, "for having by the hardshipps we underwent and living in a manner quite different from what I hade ever been accustomed to, contracted an illness which afterwards appear'd to be a fistula." Finding no one who could perform the necessary operation, he went to Charles Town and remained there three months, during which time he "was cutt three times and underwent incredible torture."

Thinking himself cured he returned to Savannah, but, alas, within a week his old ailment returned, and fearing that he could never find relief in Georgia or in South Carolina, he received permission from Oglethorpe to return to England for further treatment. And as Oglethorpe was very busy erecting his colony and was not good at writing to the Trustees to keep them posted on developments in Georgia, Gordon could now give them a first-hand report. He, thus, became the first of the Georgia colonists to make a visit back to England.

In early November he went to Charles Town on his

INTRODUCTION

way, where he was royally entertained by Governor Robert Johnson and the Council and others, and on the 25th he sailed for England, arriving in London on the 6th of January. There he received medical attention by the celebrated surgeon Dr. Chisledon (Chisleden), and was received by the Trustees, who eagerly listened to his report on Georgia.

He informed the Trustees that there were about 500 souls in Georgia, who afforded a hundred "fighting men." He praised Oglethorpe for his "indefatigable zeal in carrying on our affairs, conducting the building of the town, keeping peace, laying out of lands, supplying the stores with provisions, encouraging the fainthearted, etc.," and reported that forty houses had already been built "of timber and clapboard with shingle roofs, but Mr. Oglethorp still lay in the tent set up before the houses were built." Also, the town, standing on a bluff forty feet above high water on the river, had been fortified with twelve guns on the river front, and two blockhouses bristling with four guns each.

The "kitchen roots and herbs" which the Trustees had sent over did not do very well, and the colonists had not done a great deal of work in clearing their lands and planting crops because they busied themselves building their houses. The situation led Gordon to fear that they would not be able to maintain themselves after their year of free maintenance was out. He put great hopes in grape culture, which would give the people much employment in setting out vines, cultivating them, and harvesting the grapes for wine-making. Also he expected the silk business to thrive.

There were forty Indians living in their nearby town and they "live in great friendship with us, as we do with them." Gordon avoided telling the Trustees of the grim summer of deaths, mentioning only that "several of our people had fallen sick by drinking, as we supposed, the river water," and adding that Oglethorpe had sunk a well "in the middle of the town that produced good water, and suffitient quantity." The river was teeming with all sorts of fish, "and particularly sturgeon," and when he left Georgia "the people were healthy and orderly." [7]

To re-enforce his account of conditions in Georgia and to give the Trustees a better understanding of the new town of Savannah, Gordon produced before them at this meeting a rough sketch, showing "its situation, and manner it was laid out in, as likewise the forme and elevation of all the houses and other publick buildings." The Trustees were much pleased and ordered Gordon "to gett a compleat drawing made of it." Oglethorpe arrived in England some months later and gave Gordon additional information on that part of Savannah which had not been developed when Gordon had left, and Gordon had this information included. Oglethorpe suggested that he have the sketch printed and that it be dedicated to the Trustees. It was engraved probably in this year 1734, though the original copies show no date.

The Trustees ordered that Gordon be given sixteen guineas for his draft, which sum he called "a small present," and they further ordered that the draft be engraved. Gordon said that he had been "assisted by a subscription of many of the Honable. Trustees and other noblemen and ladies." News of this undertaking was soon back in Georgia, with some exaggeration which did not stand to Gordon's credit. Noble Jones wrote to the Trustees on July 6, 1735, "I understand Mr. Gordon Made a large Sum by his prospect of Savannah. I always thought him a Man of more Honour than to Enfringe So much on any Mans Right." Jones was inferring that Gordon

INTRODUCTION   7

had been looking over the plats which as surveyor Jones had been including in the public records in Savannah, and that Gordon before his trip to England had been copying them. Jones said that he understood that Gordon had got 100 pounds for his drawing, and this fact led Jones to be wary where he recorded his plats, so as to keep men like Gordon from plagiarizing them.[8] Thus, it might well be inferred that Gordon had been working on his rough draft before he left Savannah for England.

It is interesting to speculate on whether or not Gordon drew the finished product. He does not specifically say that he did, for, as noted above, he said that the Trustees ordered him "to gett a compleat drawing made of it." Gordon's skill as an upholsterer probably would not have fitted him to make the exquisitely drawn sketch which was engraved. It bears the title: "A View of Savannah as it stood the 29th of March, 1734. P. Gordon Inv. P. Fourdrinier Sculp. To the Honble the Trustees for establishing the Colony of Georgia in America This View of the Town of Savannah is humbly dedicated by their Honours Obliged and most Obedient Servant, Peter Gordon." Also inserted is the French title: "Vue de Savannah dans la Georgie." Objects in the View are numbered up through 15, and explanations are given at the bottom.[9]

In 1741 a print was published in London, which was a close copy of Gordon's View and frequently reproduced and often referred to as Gordon's. Evidently to keep from being labelled a plagiarism and possibly to avoid legal action, this print differed from Gordon's in that letters were used instead of numbers (and one more object was identified than in Gordon's) and the explanations were longer drawn out. Also, the number of river craft differed and were not located in the same spots, and the trees in the foreground were not in the same location. Too, there were five trees, instead of four as in Gordon's, under which Oglethorpe's tent was pitched. But the most diverting device to escape the charge of plagiarism was this entirely different wording of the title: "A View of the Town of Savanah [sic], in the Colony of Georgia in South-Carolina. Humbly Inscribed to his Excellency Genl. Oglethorpe." A cursory look at it makes it appear as Gordon's View, but on closer inspection the differences mentioned above are evident.[10] And what is quite interesting, this View is inscribed to Oglethorpe instead of to the Trustees, and equally interesting is the placing of Georgia "in South-Carolina." A partisan of South Carolina must have been responsible for this print, for by now friction had arisen between the two colonies, which later developed into attempts of South Carolina to re-incorporate Georgia as part of her territory, since at one time the territory composing Georgia had been a part of Carolina.

Gordon's appearance before the Trustees took place on February 27th, and apparently he was glad to be back in England again. Doubtless he would have been glad to remain in England and never return to Georgia, unless on a short visit, but Oglethorpe had arrived in the summer and was busy collecting additional settlers. He had brought with him the Indian King Tomochichi, with his wife, nephew, and a group of Indian chiefs and retainers. After being shown off and being royally entertained for a few months the Indians were anxious to return to Georgia, and Oglethorpe was "very desirous" that Gordon take charge of them on the ship *Prince of Wales,* which was to leave in early November (1734). Oglethorpe had been unusually kind and friendly to Gordon; the Trustees had continued him in his office as First Bailiff, and as a further token of their esteem and confidence

INTRODUCTION 9

they had provided him with two servants and were now paying the expenses of his passage and of his wife and the two servants. Captain George Dunbar, the commander, reported that Gordon and his assistant managed affairs "with So much prudence and good Sence that every thing is as orderly as cou'd be expected." [11]

Gordon, on the *Prince of Wales,* with his Indian charges reached Georgia late in December. According to his account, upon his return he found the people in an uproar, protesting against the tyrannical actions of Thomas Causton, who as keeper of the Trustees' stores was accused of charging exorbitant prices and actually trying to starve the poor people. As Third Bailiff and actually the only one of the three who took his duties seriously and held court, Causton was accused of acting the despot in his decisions. And according to Gordon, the people before his arrival had entered into a design to send Causton back to England in chains.

As might be expected, a people off the streets of London settled in a new and raw frontier found themselves almost as much out of harmony with their environment and with as little understanding of it as if they had been transported to the moon. Scarcely any of them had ever worked on a farm or even seen one; nor had they any acquaintance with what they would have to do in Georgia. The occupations of most of those who had come out on the first embarkation were not of practical use in a frontier country. The first settlers were potash makers, traders and merchants, peruke makers, calico printers, tailors, clothworkers, turners, upholsterers, basketmakers, flax and hemp workers, mercers, heelmakers, cordwainers, stockingmakers, wheelwrights, and so on. Only one farmer was listed, one gardener, and a few carpenters, all of whom would find things to do in Georgia about which they knew something—but they amounted to about a half dozen, all told. So, it was only normal to expect disappointments, murmurs, and complaints; and anyone who wanted to capitalize on this situation would find a most inviting field. Such leaders were not long in coming to the front, to assume direction of factions which were springing up, to weld together their complaints against the local government officials, and to extend complaints to the Trustees and to their whole scheme for settling Georgia. These people soon came to be called Malcontents.

One of the first factions that arose related to the case of Joseph Watson, whom the Earl of Egmont termed "an insolent vile man . . . Twice fyn'd for scandal; again fyn'd for assaulting an Indian, and afterwds. capitally convicted of killing one, but brought in lunatick." [12] To be more specific, Watson had come over to Georgia at his own expense, bringing his wife, and according to Egmont "tis said he has a grant of 500 acres, but I don't find when [where?], or when taken up." [13] He was soon in trouble, drinking too much rum and carousing with Indians in his drinking—this no doubt to further his trading with them. An Indian drinking companion of his finally died from too much indulgence, and Watson began bragging that he had drunk the Indian to death. This fact and his other associations with the red men it was feared might arouse the Indians into an uprising against the colony. He was brought before Bailiff Causton, tried in open court, and sentenced to prison as a lunatic.[14]

Among those who found great satisfaction in complaining about conditions in the Colony, and especially against the governing authorities, there soon developed the feeling that Watson was being persecuted and unjustly treated. Gordon on his return took the side of

Watson, and took the lead in harassing Causton. In a letter to the Trustees, Causton said everything was going smoothly until Gordon "unhappily, took part with Watson, and discovered to the People, that he had different Sentiments from me. They soon Concluded That as he was First Bailiff, it was in his Power to Order every thing." When Causton protested to Gordon how gently he had treated Watson in the light of his crimes, Gordon replied "That he thought it was not very gentle usage to Imprison a Man for the Sake of an Indian." Causton further informed the Trustees that Gordon had "often changed his mind in this Affair; One day he came to me and told me that Watson was a Very Villain and a Madman." [15]

Gordon thought that Watson ought to be admitted to bail,[16] and Watson's wife bestirred herself in every direction to get him released. She appealed to the Trustees, who refused to interfere with Bailiff Causton's sentence; and ultimately she appealed the case to the Privy Council in London. To prevent the British Government from interfering in their Georgia affairs, the Trustees had Watson released. Ten years later he was still in the Colony. This, the most celebrated case in Georgia's Trustee period, seems to have been the only instance when a case was appealed to the Privy Council during that time.[17]

In the meanwhile Gordon was busying himself acting the part of a man of great importance in the Colony and currying favor with all who had complaints of any sort. One supporter wrote the Trustees that Gordon's "proceedings seem to please the People. His courteous & good Nature are virtues which often gains the good Esteem & respect of all mankind & was at Church Sunday Last When another was Absent That for Some Reason might have been there." [18] And this same one, writing again, said that Gordon had "gained the Approbation of ye People."[19] The reference to the other person who was absent at Sunday church services was undoubtedly to Causton, who was being hounded by the Malcontents. He wrote the Trustees that he was disappointed in Gordon since his return from England, that he had hoped that Gordon would "save me the Trouble of Acting (on every occasion), in the Office of Magistrate," but to Causton's surprise Gordon had "encouraged complaints and Raised Discord," acting as if he had returned "with some great Commission." Nothing seemed to please Gordon, and when Causton tried to get him to specify just what it was he did not like, Causton could never pin him down to any particular; but he had "Encouraged Complaints against the Administrators of Justice, helped Vilifye, Ridicule, and oppose all former Management, hearing One Side without the other."[20]

Gordon had apparently come to the conclusion that he was the most important man in Georgia, and as he surveyed the situation he convinced himself that he must return to England to inform the Trustees how shaky their Colony was and how it might collapse at almost any time. Writing letters would not do; he must himself go; but as proof of what he would tell the Trustees he induced the complainants to write him letters setting forth their grievances. In all, seven letters were addressed to Gordon, which he would deliver to the Trustees, and there were other letters setting forth complaints, directed to the Trustees. All of these letters Gordon would take with him. Thus, he had made himself the chief agent of the Malcontents.[21]

Most of these letters contained bitter indictments against Causton, who was accused of skulduggery in the Indian trade and in his questionable dealings and rela-

INTRODUCTION 13

tions with Mary Musgrove, and also of selling rum at the Trustees' store and patronizing illegal rum houses.[22] In one of the letters "a poor unhappy Widow" appeals to Gordon for justice, which, by inference, she could not get from Causton. Her husband had been a South Carolina trader, who on a trip to Savannah had died there, leaving a cargo of merchandise including a hogshead of rum, a barrel of sugar, "and Sundry other Merchandise," which she had not been able to recover.[23] Another wanted Gordon to tell the Trustees about the bad conditions in Georgia and how tyrannical Causton was;[24] still another wanted Gordon to get permission from the Trustees for him to return to England in order to get some servants to bring back to Georgia.[25] And poor old Watson, in jail for lunacy and murdering an Indian, wanted Gordon to intercede for him before the Trustees and to plead that they rescue the people "from the unlimited Teyraney they now Groan under."[26]

Hardly more than two months after he had returned from England in late 1734, Gordon with his bale of complaints and tales of woe was planning to sail for England again; and he was undoubtedly hoping that this would be the last time he would see Georgia, for he had left his house in the care of Patrick Houstoun, a Scotsman of learning and social standing, for him to sell if possible, as well as his herd of cattle, whose cattle brand Houstoun asked Gordon to identify.[27]

In early March, 1735, Gordon went to Charles Town to dispose of some merchandise which he had brought back from England,[28] and that same month, without let of the Trustees or hindrance from anyone, he set sail for England, arriving about the first of May. As Egmont was to comment some years later, Gordon had left Georgia, "contrary to his duty and Covenant being without leave of the Trustees or acquainting them therewith. He was a conceited unstable man, and his purpose in returning, was, as it afterwards appeared, to set up a punch house in London." Being courted by Causton's enemies "pleased his vanity, and he undertook to expose their pretended grievances to the Trustees, yet never came near them till sent to," and then he delivered several complaints against Causton.[29]

Arriving in London, Gordon on May 7th addressed a long letter to the Trustees, informing them that he had decided to return to England to inform them of the serious situation that prevailed in Georgia, apparently without attempting to appear before them "til sent to." The people could not get their lands surveyed and were forced to live in town where prices were higher than they were able to pay. Some had to resort to pawning "their wearing apparell for their Subsistance." Court was being held too often. The Tythingmen, the jurors, the witnesses, "and many idle Spectators who are drawn there out of curiosity" were losing a third of their time which should have been devoted to labor. All of this interruption, when a case might last four or five days and not amount to twenty shillings! Echoing the attacks on Causton in the letters which he had brought with him, Gordon charged that Causton was a tyrant in his court, and that he promoted the sale of rum, punch, and other liquors and patronized places operating without a license. Also Tybee Light was neglected, the "poor unhappy Widow" Bowling (by name) was being cheated out of 900 pounds worth of merchandise by Causton, and the Colony was ready to collapse. He had letters to prove all these charges against Causton. He wanted the Trustees to understand that he had no "personal peek" against Causton, for he had never had "the least difference" with

INTRODUCTION 15

him. Instead, Causton had offered him the money value of the stores which were due Gordon but which he had not collected, all amounting to 20 or 30 pounds.[30]

Gordon appeared before the Trustees at their meeting on May 10th, in an atmosphere which could not have been very friendly toward him—he having left Georgia without their permission and not having honored the Trustees with a visit when he reached London until they had sent for him. Also, Oglethorpe, who was now back in England for a time, had the previous month told the Trustees that according to his last news from Savannah, there had been "a great deal of murmuring and uneasiness from the time that Gordon, our first bailiff, arrived there with the Indian chiefs, and he is of opinion that this has proceeded from Gordon, who it is suspected is a Papist." And Egmont, who was making this report, added, "This we design to enquire into, as a matter of very great consequence." [31]

Ushered in, Gordon presented "a Memorial to the Trustees," and then produced his letters of protest which he had collected in Georgia. The Trustees ordered all of the letters to be read but took no action at that time.[32] Causton, who was the principal object of attack in the letters, and had become the whipping boy for the Malcontents, wrote the Trustees "complaining of Gordon the head bailiff," and gladly offered to answer the complaints which Gordon and others had made against him.[33] Herman Verelst, Accountant and Secretary to the Trustees, wrote Causton a friendly letter in July (1735) saying that the Trustees were "very sensible of the great fatigue you have had in the Administration of Justice; and they hoped that" Gordon's return to Georgia the previous year "would have eased you in some degree of the burthen; but in that [they] have found themselves dissapointed by his not having assisted you in inforcing the Trustees Orders & quitting their Service without Licence." [34]

At a meeting of the Common Council of the Trustees on August 13th, a petition from Gordon was read "wherein he desired to have leave to sell his lands, town lot and cattle, being determined to remain in England." The Council "considered how ill he had behaved in leaving the Colony without our permission and countenancing complaints against the other magistrates, whereby the faction there received encouragement." In the light of these facts, they suspended action "until Mr. Oglethorp is returned to Georgia, and shall have enquired into his behaviour." [35] Without waiting for a report from Oglethorpe, in view of Gordon's expressed determination not to return to Georgia, and as a gesture of support for Causton and of confidence in him, the Council in September dismissed Gordon as Bailiff and appointed Causton to the position of First Bailiff.[36] At a meeting of the Trustees in October, they called Gordon in and informed him that when they heard from Oglethorpe "how the Affairs of the Colony stand in relation to the Complaints of the said Gordon, they will then consider of his Demands, but cannot before." [37]

Gordon was now without friends among the Trustees in London, and the only supporters he had in Georgia were the Malcontents. A few years later (in 1741) these Malcontents published a bitter attack on Causton (and on Oglethorpe, too), in which they misstated several facts in their praise of Gordon, saying that Causton as Bailiff ruled Georgia with an iron hand until the Trustees sent over Gordon in December, 1734, who was "a person of a very winning behaviour, affable and fluent in speech." According to the Malcontents, Gordon soon displeased

INTRODUCTION   17

Causton and Causton got rid of him "by refusing him provisions from the store, which in a little time rendered him incapable to support himself and family." [38] Egmont answered these misstatements and the book in general by saying that the authors "lye for lying sake," and then proceeded to give the facts as have already appeared in this sketch.[39]

Gordon never again returned to Georgia; [40] instead he busied himself in seeking satisfaction and redress from the Trustees. Almost two years after he had petitioned the Trustees for permission to sell his property in Georgia and "for a reward for his services," in June, 1737, the Committee to whom the petition had been referred came to a decision. They called him in "and showed him that he was so far from meriting anything from us for his services, that he had forfeited his grant by coming over without leave, contrary to his covenant in the grant, and to the neglect of his trust as first bailiff." But, "in compassion to his circumstances" they gave him leave "to sell his lot, provided it was to a person approved of by the Trustees." Also they allowed "a year's subsistence for him and his wife," which amounted to about 14 pounds; but they showed him that he owed the Trustees about 27 pounds "for so much cash advanced him, which he must account for." Gordon "pretended to know nothing about it." [41] In the following October the Common Council of the Trustees agreed to this decision.[42]

On April 12, 1738, Peter Gordon and his wife surrendered to the Trustees their property in Georgia, and proposed that it should go to Ann and Susannah Cook, daughters of William Cook. The Trustees agreed to this arrangement.[43] Cook was a major in Oglethorpe's Regiment and had lately arrived in Georgia.[44] Gordon now had few years of life left; he died in 1740, according to

Egmont, writing some years later.[45] Dead before he was forty, Gordon's life had been neither long nor apparently very satisfactory.

Gordon's Manuscript

This is a curious narrative, a mixture of short accounts in diary form, and extended excursions into criticisms of the Trustees' policies regarding land holdings and inheritance, white indentured servants and Negro slaves, and the impracticality of both the form of government for the Colony and of its personnel. Gordon begins with a short discussion of the founding of colonies by the Romans. He then gives a description of the plans and purposes of the Trustees for founding the Colony of Georgia. Next comes a diary of his voyage across the Atlantic to Charles Town, on to Port Royal, and ending at Yamacraw Bluff, where the town of Savannah was founded. He has something to say about cutting down trees and building houses, about treating with the Indians, and about conditions in Savannah as the town developed. He comments on setting up civil government there and then launches out on his hostility to the main scheme of the Trustees in developing the Colony. He mentions his first return to England, his trip back to Georgia, and ends his manuscript (as far as it is known) in the midst of a sentence.

The manuscript covers a period of about two years, beginning November 17, 1732, and ending on October 31, 1734; but as he did not arrive in Georgia until February 1, 1733 (the days of the months are in Old Style), the period of the manuscript dealing with Georgia is less than a year and eight months; and Gordon's actual residence in Georgia was almost exactly one year.

When he composed this manuscript and what his pur-

INTRODUCTION   19

pose was are not entirely clear. At the beginning of it he wrote what might appear to be an introduction or even its title: "There is now in the press, and will be published in a few days An Account of the first Setling of the Colony of Georgia. With a Journall of the Voyage of the first imbarkation, under the Direction of Mr. Oglethorp. And continued till the constitution of the Court of Record, and establishing the Governmt. of Savannah. With some account of the Magistrates. And some considerations, on the probability of Succeeding in the Said Colony, under the present Constitution, and Plann of Governmt. To which will be added the particular Case of Peter Gordon, Chief-Bailiff of Savannah, with Coppies of his Memorialls Delivered to the Honble: the Trustees and humbly offor'd to their further consideration."

His statement that the work he is describing "is now in the press, and will be published in a few days," may not be taken at face value but rather as his hope, for it seems certain from extensive and intensive research that no publication by him or one with the title he gives ever appeared. And it should be observed that the long descriptive title is an exact analysis of the narrative here under consideration, with the exception of the "Memorialls" which he says "will be added." In his narrative he makes this same statement.

This last expression would tend to confirm the belief that this manuscript was intended as a further argument and plea (in addition to his petition previously mentioned) that the Trustees do him justice in recompensing him for his services in Georgia. Their award of about 14 pounds with an offset of about 27 pounds left Gordon with much less than nothing for his services in helping to establish the Colony of Georgia. It should be noted here that the Bailiffs received no salary, but only their upkeep from the Trustees' store, which was estimated at about 14 pounds a year.

It is, of course, evident that Gordon wrote this manuscript in England after his final return in 1735, and he must have written it after the Trustees' settlement with him in April, 1738. In several places he left blank spaces for dates which he did not remember and for which he apparently at the time had no records, such as the date when the messenger arrived with the news that the Indian chiefs were coming to Savannah, and also the dates on which he embarked at Gravesend on his return to Georgia and when he arrived back there. The narrative gives unmistakable evidence that Gordon kept a diary or journal, but not throughout the whole time.

Since Gordon's narrative ends in an unfinished sentence, it would be illogical to assume that Gordon did not continue his manuscript; however, the part here under consideration is all that is known to have been found. It fills a vellum-bound book, 7¾ by 8 inches in size, and contains 90 pages. The bottom of the last page is filled with some scribbling of accounts, a fact suggesting that the book had originally been intended as an account book. This point is further emphasized by the fact that there appears on the front outside cover the title "Receipts" and some following words so dim from age as not to be decipherable.

It would seem, therefore, that the narrative was continued in a second book to include the "Memorials" as well as "some other curious letters concerning the affairs of the Colony" which Gordon promised. The complete history of the volume which has come down to the present is not known, but written on the inside front cover, in pencil, is information which carries its source back to

INTRODUCTION 21

1827: "This Book was given me by Mr [space] Oglethorps Sub Sheriff of the County of Lancaster at Lpool 22 Dec. 1827 who said it was given to him about 6 or 7 years ago by the Keeper of the Records at Chester Castle who found it at the Castle at Chester." This statement is unsigned; but at the top of this same inside cover is written in ink, "Recd from the late Richd Richardson Decr 1834 P. Maxwell." This would indicate that Richardson had received the book from the Mr. Oglethorpe referred to above.

The late Keith Read of Savannah made an impressive collection of Georgiana over a long span of his years, including especially early manuscript materials. It is not known when or from whom the Peter Gordon volume came into his possession; but when his estate was finally liquidated, that part of his Georgiana which remained was bought by the Wormsloe Foundation of Savannah in 1957 and presented to the University of Georgia. The Gordon manuscript was included in this purchase and presentation. It is now kept in the University of Georgia Library as part of the "Keith Read Manuscript Collection."[46]

In this age of enlightenment it ought not to be necessary to say that the manuscript here published has been faithfully transcribed, checked and rechecked, and edited according to the accepted standards of the day. After the idiosyncrasies of Gordon's script have been mastered, reading his manuscript is easy. In tune with his times he spelled words as the spirit moved him, sometimes using different spellings for the same word and sometimes never arriving at the modern arrangement of letters—as for instance his attempts on that water craft *pettiagua* or *pettiauger*. He liked to add an *e* to such words as *had* and *person* and *go*, and he often spelled our as *owr*. Such peculiarities have been left, as these spellings are easily understood. Many raised letters have been brought down. Though his use of capital letters creates no problem of clarity, yet it has been thought best to lower them to small letters except where modern usage would leave them. Gordon's punctuation has been changed in the interest of clarity, for often his use of commas and colons and semicolons leaves a confusion of words, without any sure signs as to where a sentence ends. The headings in the narrative were supplied by the editor. Identification of places and names of persons and explanations of certain statements and allusions have been kept to a minimum.

E. M. C.

The Journal of Peter Gordon 1732-1735

As the setling of Colony's has in all ages been esteemed a prudent, and praise worthy undertaking, so we find from many instances in history that they have often been attended with the success that such noble and generous undertakings deserved. Nor is it at all to be wondered at, that the Roman Colony's succeeded so greatly as they did, when we consider them, first, as a people unaquainted with the many vices, which are at this time, but too fashionable and generall; and almost strangers to luxury and profussion of living. Besides the Romans were a people little aquainted with traffick, and as yet arts and sciences hade made but a small progress amongst them, so that their minds were wholly bent upon improveing and cultivating their lands, as the only means they hade for their subsistance, nor hade as yet their governours any self interested views of raising private fortunes, and by that means prostituting justice, and oppressing the people to accomplish their base and unworthy ends. But on the contrary, laboured in common with the meanest, for their daily subsistance, which glorious example could not faile to inspire the breast of ever'y Roman to labour, and that with the utmost chearfulness.

This was the state of the Colony's in those dayes, and to which was owing the great progress and figure they made in the world. The case now is certainly very different, because the people generally used in setling our moderne Colony's are a people who have either by misfortunes, or ill conduct, been reduced from plenty to a state of indigency and want. Or they are the idle and abandoned part of mankind, who were ever strangers to labour and industry, and who are always ready to enter upon any undertaking where they can be supplyed with a year's provissions, their darling idleness idulg'd for some part of that time, and their minds puffed up with mighty hopes and expectations of success. But alass when they enter upon the scene of action and feel the many hardships and difficulty's, such undertakings must for ever be attended with, their industrious resolutions are intirely defeated, and they beginn to wish themselves in any other place and if that cannot be accomplish'd, they return like a dog to his vomite, to gratify those vicious habits of idleness and drinking, which brought them to that unhappy state before. Thus farr I thought necessary to say of Colony's in generall and shall now proceed to the particulars of Georgia.

1. *Plan and Purpose for Settling Georgia*

His Majesty having by his Royall Charter granted that tract of land lying between the rivers, Savanah and Altamaha, and now distinguished by the name of Georgia; to be setled and erected into a Colony and for that purpose hade approved of Trustees for carrying the project into execution. Nothing could be more conducive to the sucess of the undertaking than the choise that was made of so many worthy patriots, men distinguished for their extensive charity and benevolences to mankind to conduct and cary on the work. And who as a proof of their being intirely disinterested in the undertaking, hade at their own requestes bound themselves and their successors by the sd: Charter from receiving any benefite, what-so-ever from the sd. Colony.

The trustees, for so we must now call them, in order to be enabled to cary on so great a work, found it necessary to prepare the minds of the people for their charitable contributions, by publishing some account of their designs,[1] and sometime after, reasons for establishing said Colony.[2] Wherein was represented the excelence of the climate, the fruitfulness of the land, and the great plenty of all good things with which the country abounded, and likewise the great advantage the nation in generall would reap from such a setlemt. which was capable by that amount of producing silk and wine in such quantities, that in a short time there was the greatest reason to believe, would be able to answear our consumption, and by that means save to the nation imence sums of mony that is yearly laid out in forreign countries, for those commodities. And that at so small an expence as twenty pounds, an unfortunate family might not only be transported thither, but also put in a condition of supporting afterwards, and making a provision for posterity. Some other accounts, particularly one by Coll. Pury[3] was published about that time, wherein it was represented as the Land of Promise, overflowing with the abundance of all good things necesary and desirable for the comfortable support of life, and those to be obtained with half the labour, industry and application, that is required here for the lowest subsistance. Many were led into errors by this falacious account which has been found by experience to have very litle truth, for its foundation, seem'd to be calculated only to answear the Coll' private views; however, those accounts excited the curiosity and desire of great numbers of unfortunate people, to apply to the Trustees, to be of the number of those who should be sent in the first imbarkation, yet not withstanding the beautifull prospect that things cary'd by the accounts that were published, and the necesitious circumstances of those that applyed to the Trustees to be sent over. There were some thinking men amongst the number, who were unwilling to engage in the affair, before they were informed of the tenure by which they were to hold their lands, and of severall other circumstances relating to the Governement Consititution of the intended Colony.

To the first of which they were told by the Trustees that no larger quantity thane fifty acres was to be given to any one persone sent over and assisted with a years provissions at the publick expence. Nor any quantity exceeding five hundred acres to any persone that should goe at their own expence to setle there, and cary with them the number of servants to occupy the land as is requir'd by their grant. That their lands were lyable to severall forfeitures, and that in case of dying without male issue their lands were to revert to the Trustees. This gave occassion, to one of the people, who hade engaged to goe over in the first imbarkation, to represent to the Trustees, that as he hade only one child and that a daughter he could by no means think of going upon those terms, alledging that his daughter being equally dear to him as a sone, he could never enjoy eny peace of mind, for the apprehension of dying there, and leaving his child, destitute and unprovided for, not having a right to inherite or posses any part of his reall estate, or the improvements that he hade made upon it either by industry or expending the litle substance he hade brought from England with him for that purpose.

The Trustees, in consequence of this objection were pleased to indulge the first imbarkation, with the priviledge of nominating their heirs, male or female, related, or otherwise. This condesention of the Trustees, removed many of the difficulties, that were started by the first imbarkation, with regard to themselves. Tho there still remain'd great uneasiness amongst them, with regard to their posterity. For tho the Trustees hade given them the priviledge of naming their successors; yet as that was to be no law, and regarded only the first setlers they consider'd that their posterity, would find themselves in a much worse situation, by their estates reverting to the Trustees, in failure of male issue with all the improvements made upon it till the time of such revertion. And that tho the Trustees hade likewise assured them that upon any persons dying without male issue, and the next of kinn applying to them the right of inheritance should be given to him, provided that; he would occupy the same himself. Or otherwise, that they would give to the next heir applying, a consideration equall to the value of the said lands and improvements. Tho these promises were made by the Trustees yet they were not suffitient to remove the apprehensions of the people. Because they looked upon them, as things of courtisie only. And not such as they hade a right to claime, by the laws, and Consititution of the Colony; besides they considered, that tho the present Trustees were gentlemen of unblemished honour, and unspotted characters, yet they were mortall and in case of death, might be succeeded, by others, who would act upon quite different principles, and who instead of doeing justice, and adhearing to the rules and designs of the worthy gentlemen they succeeded, might have nothing in view but the pursuite of their own interests, by disposing of the lands and improvements, of those who should happen to die, and who hade ventured their lives [and] litle fortunes in making of their setlements, amongst their own friends and relations.

Nor were they at any certainty upon what terms they were to hold their lands, at the expiration of twenty years, when the deed of Trust granted by the King to the Trustees, expired, which was likewise a very great uneasiness to them. Yet not withstanding they chearfully sign'd an instrument prepar'd by order of the Trustees for that purpose whereby they oblidg'd themselves not to quitt the Colony in less thane three years without leave first obtain'd of the Chief Person in Power. That their labour should be in common till they hade erected houses sufficient for the whole and rais'd some other publick buildings for the service of the Colony, after which they received orders to repair on board of shipp, who thane lay at Gravesend, by the 9th of Nov. [1732]. At the same time the Reverd: Mr. [Samuel] Smith, one of the Trustees, made an excelent exhortation to the people, recomending to them in the strongest and most moving terms, brotherly love, friendshipp and sobriety.

2. *The Voyage across the Atlantic*

Friday Nov. ye 17th, about eight in the morning we sail'd from Gravesend, on board the shipp Ann [also spelled *Anne*], Captain Thomas, Comander, bound for South Carolina, having on board 41 men, 27 women, and 28 children.[4] The same day about noon we came to anchor, at the Bay of the Nore, with the wind at N. B. W. [north by west]. The 18th we weighed anchor, about five in the morning, with a fine gale, and gott into the Downs about noon, where we lay by to take in fresh provissions for Mr. Oglethorps [5] use, which came on board. About three in the afternoon we thene bore away. Wind at N. In the evening we gott a breast of the South Foreland, and stood down chanell all night; in the morning the 19th the wind coming short, we stood in to the Downs again where we came to anchor, about eleven oclock. And being Sunday hade Divine Service, and a sermon preached by the Reverd. Doctor Herbert [6] who went as a voluntier in the expedition. About three in the afternoon, the wind coming about fair, we weighed anchor again and stood down chanell. The 20th were a breast of Beachy Head, with the wind at N. B. E. The 21st in the morning were a breast of the Isle of White [Wight] with a topsail gale at N. B. W. In the afternoon Mr. Warrens [7] sone was baptis'd by the name of Georgia Marino, and Mr. Oglethorp having appoynted two Constables viz. Mr. Parker [8] and Mr. Fitzwalter,[9] ordered them to stand godfathers to the child, and Mr. Hodges's [10] daughter godmother, Reverd. Doctor Herbert, making an exhortation suitable to the occassion. Afterwards Mr. Oglethorp ordered five gallons of brandy to be made into a flipp which being equally divided was three quarts to each mess which consisted of five people, and to each mess was allowed half a fowl, with bacon, and greens, which was a very agreeable refreshment, our people having never been used to salt provisions before. The evening was spent, with mirth, and order and success to the intended Collony, and the Trustees. Healths went round chearfully.

The same afternoon, about four oclock we took our departure from Beverly Point, bearing N. About five leagues distant, in the evening Mr. Huges [11] was taken ill, with fitts. The 26th about six in the morning Mr. Canons [12] child about eight months old was found dead in the bed, and the same day about five oclock the child was putt in a wooden box, and buried in the sea, Doctor Herbert performing the prayers proper for the occassion. The 28th Mr. Oglethorp sent for me to the cabins, and told me that for the better regulation of our people, he hade besides the two Constables, appoynted four Tything Men, and that the Trustees hade been pleas'd to name me for the first, and desired that I should chuse which family's I best approv'd of to be in my Tything, and under my care, which I accordingly did. Our principle bussiness on board was to see that in the serving out of the provissions and other refreshments, (which was done, every day), each family, or mess, hade justice done them, and likewise that they should come regularly, and in their turns, to be serv'd and take particular care that no cursing, swearing, or any other indeceny's should be comitted. And to prevent the danger of fire, by having candles between decks in the night, Mr. Kilbery [13] was appoynted Corporall, and to see that all the candles between decks were putt out ever'y night at eight oclock. And in case that any of the passengers should be suddenly taken ill, a watch was appoynted, of our own young men, who took it in their turns ever'y night to attend in the steerage with a lanthorne and candles.

Dec. ye 9th Mr. Hughes hade the misfortune of breaking his great toe, by the overturning of a scrutore [14] in the cabine which was emediately sett by Doctor Cox,[15] our surgeon, who made a perfect cure of it in a short time. This evening I was taken ill, and continued so till the 21st, which was Mr. Oglethorps birth day, upon which occassion, a sheep and some other fresh provissions was dress'd for our people, and a quantity of liquor given to drink the health of the day. After dinner we were diverted with cudgell playing and riding of skimingtons on account of Mrs. Coles [16] having beat her husband. At night I hade a returne of my distemper, which continued till we came upon the coast of America. During my illness I received the utmost civilities from Mr. Oglethorp, Doctor Herbert, Captain Scott,[17] and Captain Thomas, who all of them visited me constantly, and supplyed me with ever'y thing that was in their power, or wines and other refreshments.

3. Charles Town and Port Royal

Jan: ye 13th [1733] about nine in the morning we see two sails of shipps, and soon after we made land and stood for it, which we discovered in a short time to be Charles Town. Mr Oglethorp sent for me, and desired to know if my cloaths were on board, and if I could conveniently come at them, for that he intended to send me ashore with his complements to the Governour, and to bring of [off] a pilote. But being advised to fire guns, which is the usuall signall for pilotes to come off, and that it would give us the greater dispatch, it was accordingly done, but no pilote coming, Mr. Oglethorp resolved to goe himself, and sett off emediately from the shipp in the pinnace with six rowers, Mr. Amatiss,[18] Mr. Kilbery, and two servants —about six he arrived at Charlestown, and returned on board the next day at noon, and brought with him Mr. Midletone one of the pilots belonging to the men of warr, stationed at Carolina.

This day we catched plenty of dog fish, black fish, angell fish, and severall other sorts, suffitient for all the people for severall dayes which was a welcome refreshment, they having lived chiefly upon salt provissions the whole voyage. At night about eleven oclock, we weighed anchor for Port Royall, but the wind coming short, we turned to the windward all night; and in the morning being the 15th found we hade only gained four leagues. The 17th about two in the afternoon, we were alarmed by a sloop who as soon as he perceived us standing along shore, emediately changed his course and bore down upon us, which looking very suspitious made us conclude that he must either be a pirate or Spanish Guard de Costa and that his intention was to plunder us, upon which Mr. Oglethorp [19] order'd all our men upon deck, and the small arms to be brought up, and all the women and children to keep below, and not appear upon deck. In the mean time, while we were drawing our men up, and getting our arms loaded, and ready for our defence, Captain Thomas who commanded the shipp order'd his great guns to be charged, and all things ready on his part, continuing still our courss. And the sloop bearing still down upon us and who by this time hade gott so near us that we could perseive he hade Jack Ensigne and pennant flying, which appear'd to us to be Spanish Colours, but being by this time pretty well provided for him, the Captain ordered the courss to be hauled up in order to waite for him. As soon as he came within gun shott of us, the Captain order'd a gun to be fired across his stem, and we could perceive the ball to fall about a hundred yards a head of him, but that not bringing him too, as we expected it would, he ordered another to be fired, still nearer to him, which fell within a very small distance of him, upon which and fearing the next shott would be aboard him he thought proper to lower his top sails, and upon viewing us and finding we were so well provided for him both sides of the shipp being compleatly lined with armed men, he thought proper to gett upon a wind, and stand away the same courss he was in when we perceived him first. The pilote whome we hade on board said he hade some knowledge of him that he hade been a pirate, and that he certainly would have plundered us hade he not found we were too strong for him. I cannot here omitt taking notice of the bravery of some of our women who when we expected every moment to come to an ingagemt. beg'd they might be assisting in handing us up arms amunitions, and what ever should be wanted, and that if it would be permitted they would come upon deck and fight as long as they could stand, while some of our men who hade been noted the whole voyage for noisy bullying fellows, were not to be found upon this occassion but sculked either in the hold or between decks.

The 18th came to an anchor in Port Royall river. The same evening Mr. Kilbery was sent to an island in the mouth of the river to gett what canoes he could, and returned to the shipp in the evening with one canoe and two men. The next morning Mr. Oglethorp and Doctor Herbert went up the river in the pinace to Beauford Town to provide periagaes [20] to be assisting to us in debarking, and Captain Scott went with a party of six armed men in the canoe which was brought on board the night before, to secure those periagaes for owr use in their returne home who hade been imployed in carrying the Swiss under the command of Coll: Pury to their new setlement of Purisbourgh [Purrysburgh] up Savannah River; and likewise to gett hutts built for owr accomodation in owr passage to Georgia. The same day sent owr boat with the pilote to find owr anchor, which we were obligd to leave on Port Royall Barr. The day before in the evening they returned, and brought the anchor with them, but the wind being contrary, we could not gett up the river that night.

Saturday morning the wind being fair, we weighed anchor, but it coming very hazy, were obligd to come too again. Clearing up in the afternoon we weighed again, and came to our moorings about five in the afternoon, within three miles of Beauford Town. About eight in the evening a canoe was sent on board by Mr. Oglethorp to let the Captain know that he intended to come on board with the first of the tide of ebb. About eleven oclock at night he arrived, and brought with him a large periagoe, ordered severall more to attend us the next morning, when we begane early to pack up our goods, in order for a generall debarkation. About noon, we were all safely landed at the new fort where we found by Mr. Oglethorps direction the barracks belonging to Captain Massys [Philip Massey] Independant Company clean'd out on purpose for owr reception, fires lighted, and provissions provided for owr refreshment. During owr stay here which was ten dayes, we were constantly visited by the planters of the country and diverted ourselves with fishing and shooting. Here our Tythings begane to mount guard. On Sunday we hade an excellant sermone preach'd by the Reverd: Mr. Jones, minister of Beauford, under a tent which wee erected for that purpose, and likewise another adjoyning to it for the intertaining of the strangers of the better sort. Tuesday the 30th of Janry. we begane about four in the morning to pack up our goods and putt them on board petiagores in order to proceed for Georgia. About eight we were loaded and under saile, but the tide being farr spent, and it blowing very hard we were oblidged to bear a way for a creek near a place call'd the look out, where we anchor'd and lay all night. Wednesday morning, about five we weighed anchor again, with a fair wind, and arrived at Jones's Island about six in the evening where we found hutts provided for us by Captain Scotts party. The same day the Indian hunters brought us in thirteen quarters of venison which was divided amongst us and dress'd for supper.

4. Arrival at Yamacraw Bluff; Development of Savannah

Next morning being the first of February,[21] we sailed from Jones's Island, with a fair wind and arrived the same day at Yamacra Bluff in Georgia, the place which Mr. Oglethorp hade pitched upon for our intended setlement. As soon as we came near the Bluff, we were saluted by Captain Scott and his party, with their small arms, which we returned. And as soon as we landed, we sett emediately about getting our tents fixed, and our goods brought ashore, and carryed up the Bluff, which is fourty foot perpendicular height above by water mark. This by reason of the loos sand, and great height, would have been extreamly troublesome hade not Captain Scott and his party built stairs for us before our arrivall, which we found of very great use to us in bringing up our goods.

About an hour after our landing, the Indians came with their King, Queen, and Mr. Musgrave,[22] the Indian trader and interpreter, along with him to pay their complements to Mr. Oglethorp, and to welcome us to Yamacraw. The manner of their aproach was thus, at a litle distance they saluted us with a voly of their small arms, which was returned by our guard and thane [then] the King, Queen, and Chiefs and other Indians advanced and before them, walked one of their generalls, with his head adorned with white feathers, with ratles in his hands (something like our casternutts) to which he danced, observing just time, singing and throwing his body into a thousand different and antike postures. In this manner they advanced to pay their obedience to Mr. Oglethorp, who stood at a small distance from his tent, to receive them. And thane conducted them into his tent, seating Tomo Chachi[23] upon his right hand [and] Mr. Musgrave, the interpreter, standing between them. They continued on conference about a quarter of an hour, and thane, returned to their town, which was about a quarter of a mile distant from the place where we pitched owr camp, in the same order as they came. Not being able to compleate the pitching of our tents this night, and I being but lately recover'd from my illness, went to ly at the Indian town, at Mr. Musgrove, the interpreters house, with Doctor Cox and his family and Lieutenant Farringtone belonging to Captain Massy's Company, who hade order'd a handsome supper to be provided for us at Mr. Musgraves house.

As soon as the Indians were informed that we were come to Musgroves house, they begane to entertain us with dancing round a large fire which they made upon the ground, opposite to the Kings house. Their manner of dancing is in a circle, round the fire, following each other close, with many antick gestures, singing and beating time, with their feet and hands to admiration. One of the oldest of our people, Doctor Lyons, having slept away from our camp and gott a litle in drink, found his way up to the Indian town and joyned with the Indians in their dance indeavouring to mimick and ape them in their antick gestures, which I being informed of, sent for him, and desired that he would emediately repair home to our camp. Otherwise I assured him I would aquaint Mr. Oglethorp with his folly. He promised me that he would. But being so much in liquor he returned again to the Indians and danced with them as before, which being told to me I ordered severall white men who were there to carry him home by force, it being of a very bad concequence that the Indians should see any follies or indiscretions in owr old men, by which they judge that our young men must be still guilty of greater, for they measure mens understanding and judgement according to their years.

Friday the 2d we finished our tents, and gott some of our stores on shore. The 3d we gott the petiagores unloaded, and all the goods brought up to the Bluff. Sunday the fourth, we hade Divine Service performed in Mr. Oglethorps tent, by Reverd: Doctor Herbert with thanksgiving for our safe arrivall. Mr. Musgrove, the Indian trader, and his wife were present, and Tomo Chachi, the Indian King, desired to be admitted, which Mr. Oglethorp readily consented to and he with his Queen were seated in the tent. During the time of Divine Service, severall of the Indian warriors and others sate at a small distance from the tent, upon trees, and behaved very decently.

Munday the 5th Coll. Bull,[24] being a gentlemen of great experience in making of setlements, was appoynted by the Governour and Councill of Carolina to come to us to be assisting with his advise, arrived in his own periagore from Charles Town and brought severall letters for Mr. Oglethorp from the Governour and Councill.

Wednesday the 7th we begane to digg trenches for fixing palisadoes round the place of our intended setlement as a fence in case we should be attacked by the Indians, while others of us were imployed in clearing of the lines, and cutting trees to the proper lengths, which was the 14 foot for the palisadoes. About noon a fire broke out in the guard room, which instantly consumed the same, and burnt severall chests that were in it belonging to owr people and likewise a hutt adjoyning to it belonging to Mr. Warren, whose things were likewise burned. It was with much diffuculty we gott the powder out of Mr. Oglethorps tent, which stood almost joyning to the fire, and which we preserved by taking it emediately down. After we hade gott the fire pretty near extinguished, one of the large pine trees near 100 foot high took fire and to prevent further damage we were obliged to cutt it down, and in the fall it broke too barrells of beef and one barrell of strong bear [beer] in pieces and damaged the end of one of owr tents. The whole damage amounted to about twenty pounds sterling.

Thursday the 8th each family hade given out of the stores, an iron pott, frying pan, and three wooden bowls, a Bible, Common Prayer Book, and Whole Duty of Man. This day we were taken of [off] from the palisadoes and sett about sawing and splitting boards eight foot long in order to build clapp board houses, to gett us under better cover till our framed houses could be built. This evening Mr. St. Julien,[25] Mr. Whitaker, Major Barnwell, and Mr. Woodward arrived from Charlestown.

Friday our arms were delivered to us from the store viz. a musket and bayonett, cartrige box and belt to each persone able to cary arms. Sunday we were drawn up under owr arms for the first time, being divided into four Tythings, each Tything consisting of ten men, of which I was appoynted to command the first; Mr. Causton,[26] the second; Mr. Jones,[27] the third; and Mr. Goddard[28] the fourth. I mounted the first guard at eight oclock at night, received orders from Mr. Oglethorp to fix two Centinells at the extream parts of the town who were to be relieved ever'y two hours and thane returning to the guard house, which we hade built of clapp boards, upon the most convenient part of the Bluff, for commanding the river both wayes. The next night at eight oclock I was relieved by Mr. Causton, who march'd to the guard house with his Tything under arms where I received him with my Tything drawn up before the guard with their arms rested.

5. *Conditions in Savannah*

Not withstanding that our guard duty was ever'y fourth night, yet we went directly from the guard to work in the woods, after owr names were called over, which was done ever'y morning at six oclock before Mr. Oglethorps tent, and if any persone did not at that time answear to his name, except hindred by sickness, was cutt of [off] from his dayes allowance of a pint of Madeira wine, which was allowed to every working man. About this time wee hade excessive hard rains and almost continued thunder and lightening to a most astonishing degree. The rains were so violent, and came with such force, that it beat thro. our tents to that degree that we have been wett to the skinn in them severall times in a day. And to prevent our bedding from being wett, hade no other methode but by covering them with plates, dishes, bowls, and what other conveniency we hade to catch the rain in, which has often been so heavy that severall gallons has been catched in those vessells upon one bed, in the space of an hour.

As the country all round us was a continued forrest, and nothing to be seen but wood and water, the rains were very frequent and very severe. But as our people who were daily imployed in cutting down trees, and clearing the place which was intended for the town, advanced in their work, and hade cleared a pretty large space of ground, wee could perceive the rains not to be so frequent, nor so violent. Munday Mr. Oglethorp being informed that two fellows who hade broke out of Charles Town jayle, were in our neighbourhood, and hade killed severall catle, at Musgrave, the Indian traders cow penn, ordered two men with a large swivell gunn to watch near the side of the river all night to stopp their canoe in case they should attempt to pass, and if apprehended each man was to have a reward of ten pound cur. [currency] from Mr. Oglethorp. The same evening Mr. Oglethorp desired us to draw up a letter of thanks to Mr. Whitaker and the other gentlemen, who hade generously made us a present of 100 head of catle to be equally divided amongst us. We drew the letter up, and had it signed by severall of our people, and went in a body and delivered it to Mr. Whitaker and the other gentlemen.

Tuesday early in the morning wee were all ordered under arms to salute those gentlemen before they sett out for Charles Town, which we did as they were going in to their boats, with three generall discharges and three husass. The same morning we see at a distance up the river, something like a canoe, which we supposed to be the two fellows who hade made their escape from Charles Town. Upon which Mr. Oglethorp ordered me to take two men along with me, in a canoe, and goe in quest of them. I chose Mr. Cristie [29] and Mr. Cameron [30] to goe along with me, and when we came to the place where we expected to find the fellows, we found that what appeared to us in town like a boate was a large tree floating down the river. Upon which we returned.

The 18th a servant maid belonging to Mr. Hughes was ordered to be brought before Captain Scott, Conservator of the Peace, where she was accused of a loose disorderly behaviour, and endeavouring to seduce severall other young women in the Colony, upon which she was ordered to be whipt at the carts taile, and returned to England to her friends, and in the mean time she was given in charge to the Constable. The 19th Mr. Oglethorp went in the scoutt boat to the Island Tybe in the mouth of our river to pitch upon a proper place for a small setlement for some people from Carolina who desired to be admitted under his protection, and to serve as a look out for our setlement. About four in the afternoon Coll. Pury arrived at the Indian town in a canoe from Purrisbourgh. I was ordered to take four of my guard with their arms, and waite upon the Coll. with the complements of the gentlemen and to give him an invitation to our camp.

The Coll. returned their complements with great civility and desired me to aquaint the gentlemen that he would waite upon them presently. We were thane ordered all under arms, and when the Coll. arrived we saluted him with a generall discharge of our small arms. About seven in the evening Mr. Oglethorp returned in the scoutt boat from Tybe. This day our new crane was putt up.

Tuesday the 20th a warrant from Captain Scott came directed to me to see the sentence executed on the servant maid who some dayes before, was ordered to be whipt, upon which I ordered four of my guard under arms to bring her out, a negroe being appoynted to whipp her. As soon as she was brought to the cart severall of our people interceded with Mr. Oglethorp in her behalf, who remitted that part of her sentence and sent her the same day out of the Collony onboard a petiagore bound for Charles Town in the care of Mr. Osbourne,[31] the patroon. The 21st about two in the morning Doctor Herbert sett out for Charles Town, in the scoutt boat, accompanied by Coll. Pury and some of his people. The same day Mr. Kilbery sett out with a small party and an Indian guide, to apprehend the fellows who were in the woods, and hade been discovered by the Indians. About eleven at night he returned with the prisoners, who were emediately examined before Mr. Oglethorp. One of them was English and the other a French man. The Frenchman denied all he was charged with, of having broke out of Charlestown jayle, and having committed severall roberies, and killed severall catle, in our neighbourhood. The English man confess'd most of what he was charged with, alledging that what catle they killed was only for their own subsistance, they having been in a most miserable way destitute of any manner of food in the woods, and must have inevitably perished hade they not done it. The French man was ordered into custody of the guard belonging to Captain Massy's Independant Company, ten of whome with a serjeant, were ordered to be assisting to us in Georgia. The other was ordered into custody of our guard.

The 22d. Mr. Fitzwalter, one of our people, arrived with fifty head of catle and other stores from Carolina. This catle was part of the hundred, which Mr. Whitaker and his friends hade made a present of to us. The 23d. the bell was hung at the end of the crane. The 25th the two prisoners were putt on board Captain Andersons [32] petiagore to be sent to Beauford, and there to be delivered to Captain Watts, who was the commanding officer, and to be by him forwarded to Charles Town. The same day Mr. Oglethorp, Coll. Bull, and Tomo Chachi went up the river in order to give the Indians possesion of the lands alloted for their setlement, lying between the creeks six miles above us. About seven in the evening they returned to the camp. March ye 1st the first house in the square was framed, and raised, Mr. Oglethorp driving the first pinn. Before this we hade proceeded in a very unsetled manner, having been imployed in severall different things such as cutting down trees, and cross cutting them to proper lengths, for clapp boards. And afterwards splitting them into clapp boards, in order to build us clapp board houses, which was the first design, but that not answearing the expectation, we were now divided into different gangs, and each gang had their proper labour assign'd to them and to be under the direction of one persone of each gang so that we proceeded in owr labour, much more regular thane before, there being four setts of carpenters, who hade each of them a quarter of the first ward, alloted to them to build, a sett of shingle makers, with proper people to cross cutt and splitt, and a suffitient number of negroe sawyers, who were hired from Carolina to be assisting to us. The same night, one redman, an Irish man, was ordered into custody of the guard on suspition of his being a spy and intending to goe to St. Augustine, a Spanish setlement, to informe them of the situation of owr affairs. But after frequent examinations, and nothing appearing against him, he was discharged.

Sunday the fourth, after Divine Service, we were ordered under arms, and the Tythings marched regularly into the wood, a small distance from the town, where Mr. Oglethorp ordered a mark to be fixed up, at a hundred yards distance to be shott at by all the men, and who ever shott nearest the mark, to have a small prise of seven or eight shillings value. This custome which was intended to train the people up to firing, and to make them good marksmen, was generally observed, for many Sundays afterwards. That being the only day we could be possibly spared from labour, and with some success. Thursday the 7th the Indian King & Chi. [Chiefs] desired a talk with Mr. Oglethorp, which he readily granted, and received them at a house which was fitted up on purpose for that occassion. Mr. Oglethorp being seated at the door, on a bench covered with blew cloath with Captain Scott on his right hand and Mr. Jon. Brian [33] on his left, the Indians advancing with Mr. Musgrove, their interpreter, before them. Most of them hade their heads adorned with white feathers, in token of peace, and friendshipp. Before the King and other Chiefs, marched two warriors carrying long white tubes, adorned with white feathers, in their left hands, and ratles in their right hands, which was cocoa nutt shells, with shott in them, with which they beat time to their singing as they marched along, but before they reached where Mr. Oglethorp was they made severall stopps, and at each stopp they begane a new song, in which they recounted all the warlike exploits of their forefathers, which is all the records they have, and the only methode of handing down to posterity the history of their great men. When they came near the place where Mr. Oglethorp was, the two warriors, who carried the feathers, and ratles in their hands, advanced before the King and other Chiefs singing and playing with their ratles and putting themselves in many antike postures. Thane, they came up to Mr. Oglethorp and the other gentlemen and waved the white wings they carried in their hands, over their heads, at the same time singing and putting their bodys in antike postures. Afterwards they fixed a lighted pipe of tobaco to the tubes which they held in their hands, and presented it to Mr. Oglethorp, who having smoaked severall whiffs they thane presented it to the other gentlemen, who observed the same methode which Mr. Oglethorp hade done. Thane they afterwards presented the same pipe to their King and two of their Chiefs, the King and each of the Chiefs smoaking four whiffs, blowing the first whiff to the left, the next to the right, the third upwards, and the fourth downwards. After this ceremony was over, they walked in to the house, the King being seated opposite to Mr. Oglethorp and the Chiefs on his right hand, thane Mr. Oglethorp desired the interpreter to ask the King, whether they desired to speak first. The King said they did, and bid the interpreter should say to Mr. Oglethorp, that they were glade to see him, and his people, safely arrived in this country and bid us hearty welcome to Yamacraw. Thane he said that with regard to one of his people, that hade been killed by the Uchis [Uche, Uchee] (another neighbouring nation of Indians) he would not take revenge without Mr. Oglethorps concent and approbation, (taking revenge is a terme they use, when they intend to declare warr). He thane said that he was not a stranger to the English, for that his father and grand father had been very well known to them. He afterwards presented Mr. Oglethorp with some deer skins, which is the most valuable, and indeed the only thing of value they have. Mr. Oglethorp after having assured them of his friendshipp, and utmost assistance and protection, made them some presents with which they were very much pleased. They afterwards returned to their own town in the same manner as they came.

Wee hade hither too continued very healthy, and proceeded in the publick labour with as much success and dispatch as could possibly be expected. But the weather beginning to be extreamly hott, and owr people haveing as yet no other water to drink but that of the river, which at high water was brackish, we did not long enjoy that happiness, for soon afterwards we begane to be very sickly, and lost many of owr people who died very suddenly.

Aprile the 6th Doctor Cox died very much lamented, being a generall loss to the Collony. He was a very useful and well experienced gentlemen. As the first persone that died, and we being thane, under a sort of a military government Mr. Oglethorp ordered that he should be buried in a military manner. All owr Tythings were accordingly ordered to be under arms, and to march regularly to the grave, with the corps, and as soon as he was interr'd and the funerall service performed we gave three generall discharges of owr small arms and during the time that we marched with the corps, and while the funerall office was performing, minute guns were fired from the guard house and the bell constantly toling. This military manner of burying was afterwards observed not only to all owr men that died, but likewise to owr women, till the people begane to die so fast that the frequent firing of the canon, and owr small arms, struck such terrour, in owr sick people (who knowing the cause, concluded they should be the next) that we have hade three or four die in one day which being represented to Mr. Oglethorp he ordered that it should be discontinued.

The Reverd: Mr. Quincy [34] arrived from England, and succeeded the Reverd: Doctor Herbert, who some time before was returned but died in his passage. We hade now found out a spring of water, about half a mile distant from the town, which was of great service to the people. Soon after we discovered severall more. But to prevent the trouble of going so farr to fetch it Mr. Oglethorp ordered a well to be sunk in the midle of the town, not expecting to find water in less thane 40 or 50 foot. However before they hade sunk 25 foot we found plenty of water, which still continues to supply the town.

Mr. Oglethorp sett out in the scout boat for Charles Town in South Carolina, in order to apply to the Governour and Assembly, for some assistance towards carrying on the Colony, which having succeeded in, returned to Savanah, and brought severall gentlemen along with him to visit owr new Collony. During his absence an unlucky accident hade like to have hapned. Captain Scott to whome the command of the place was left, the civill govermt. not being yet sttd. [settled], having ordered a servant belonging to one Gray [35] to attend him and the rest of the gentlemen that came to visit the Collony, Gray refused to send him, alledging that it was a very great hardship to have his property taken from him, which he looked upon his servant to be, and having infused this notion amongst the common people with whome he conversed, had formed a larg faction, who all agreed not to part with the servant, but would rather lose their lives in protecting him. This being whispered about, Captain

Scott sent to me at night, when I went to relieve the guard and desired that I should take a file of my guard, with their arms, and goe and demand the servant, and bring him away. I accordingly chose two of the people I could best trust so, and came to the house where the servant was, but could not gett admittance for some time. At length the door was opened, and I went in with my men and demanded the servant, which the master refused, and the women who were in the house declared that there were twenty arm'd men without, ready to defend him in case any attempt was made to take him away by force. I told them the necesity I was under of obeying command, without no good order could possibly subsist, that tho I was determined not to goe without the servant, yet I was very unwilling to carry things to extreamity, and assured them that there was no intention of taking the servant from them, only to be assisting for a few dayes till Mr. Oglethorps returne, when I told them they might depend upon having any grievance redress'd as soon as he arrived. And their conduct in submitting to command, very much approved of, still I could not prevaille, by all the fair means I could possibly use, [convince them] so I resolved to carry it a litle farther, and with some small litle opposition I gott upstairs where the servant was, and ordered him to come down emediately, which with some reluctance he obey'd. But still the difficulty was to gett him out of the house, for they begane to be very clamorous, and sounded still resolved not to part with him. And I on the other hand was determined not to goe without him. And once more begg'd they would consider the concequence of opposing authority, that it would be deem'd mutiny and that they certainly would be punished as such, and at the same time assured them that if they would let the servant goe peaceably, in obedience to command, I gave them my word he should be returned to them in an hours time, and likewise promised that he should not receive any punishment. This at last they agreed to, and according to my promise the servant was returned in an hours time. So we happily gott over this affair which might have been attended with very fatall concequences.

6. *Treating with the Indians*

On the [blank space] a messenger arrived with an account that the Chiefs of the Upper Creeks and Uchi nations were arrived at Captains Bluff in their way to Savanah, upon which a house was ordered to be fitted up to receive them in, and the next morning they arived in a petiagore, having travell'd five hundred miles thro the woods to enter in to a Treaty of Friendshipp with Mr. Oglethorp, and receive the presents usuall on those occassions. There was to conduct them two Indian traders and interpreters, whom Mr. Oglethorp had sent up to the nations on purpose to bring them down. As soon as they arrived Mr. Oglethorp ordered me to goe to the water side and receive them at their landing, which I did and conducted them to the house where Mr. Oglethorp was to receive them. And Mr. Oglethorp being willing to show them owr strength, the great guns were fired as soon as they landed, which they seem'd much surprised at, many of them having never heard a cannon before, and all owr people being under arms lined the way on each side they were to pass thro from the Bluff to the house where Mr. Oglethorp was.

The Kings or Chiefs were seated on each side of Mr. Og. [Oglethorpe] and the interpreters stood before, and the other Indians about four score in number satt on the floor, smoaking tobaco, and Mr. [John] Colleton and Mr.

St. Julien, two gentlemen who came to visit us from Carolina, filled wine and were assisting during the time of the talk, which being ended, and they having received their presents, they retired each nation to a different camp, a small distance from the town where they continued a week, and were supply'd during that time with provissions from the Trustees stores.

7. Civil Government Setup

About this time Mr. Oglethorp haveing some thoughts of returning to England, as soon as he could possibly gett things a litle setled and being desirious before his departure, to see what success the new scheme of government would have, declared his intentions of constituting the court (which was to be a Court of Record) and qualifying those persones who were appoynted to the magistracy, by a speciall comission from the Trustees before we left England, with (as it was believed) a discretionary power to continue or discontinue them as he found they were deserving. Accordingly the day was appoynted which was the 7th of July [1733], when the people being assembled together Mr. Oglethorp opened the Trustees Commission for appoynting the magistrates, and called and qualified them according to their rank, which was as follows: Peter Gordon, first Bailiff; William Waterland,[36] second; Thomas Causton, third; Thomas Christie, Recorder; and Joseph Hughes, Register. The goverment. of owr new setlement being thus modell'd, wee were now to act in a sphere different from any thing wee hade ever appear'd in before, the nature of which wee were but too litle aquainted with; and I cannot help saying not suffitiently qualified for offices of so great power and trust, as the disposall of such a number of peoples libertyes and properties, and even their lives, in as full a sense as any judge in England as has been suffitiently evidenced by severall instances.

The other inferior officers, such as Constables and Tything men, were to be appoynted occasionally by the magistrates as they found it necesary. And now all matters both civill and criminall were to be determined before the Court, which as I observed before, consisted of the magistrates I have already mentioned, with a jury of twelve freholders, who were to be properly summoned for that duty by the Recorder or Town Clerk.

This forme of governmt. seem'd to be agreable enough to the people, who were generally satisfied with the decissions of the Court, in the litle matters, either about property or otherwise, which hade as yet been brought before them, but when they considered them as a sett of men, in whose hands and power their lives and fortunes were intrusted and that tho they should be ever so much oppress'd or aggrieved, there was no redress to be expected but by an application to the Trustees in England, which by reason of the distance, was looked upon as a tedious and uncertain relief, besides the danger of having their conplaints rejected, and the representations of the people in power (against whome their complaints might probably be justly grounded) receiv'd by the Trustees, which consequently could not faile to throw them under their displeasure and make them be looked upon as a turbulant and restless people, for in the setling of Col. [Colony] I say when they came to view the magistrates therefor in this light they begane thane naturally to reflect upon the qualifications and characters of those people who were thuss intrusted with the governmt. of the Colony; and finding that tho they were men of fair reputation, yet as they hade never made the law's of their country their study and were almost as litle aquainted with them as they were themselves (nay some pretended to a much superior knowledge of the laws thane any persone in the administration), they therefor by no means looked upon them as people of concequence enough or suffitiently qualified for so great a trust as was reposed in them.

This naturally produced a disregard both for them and their proceedings and tho they could only express their dislikes in privatt caballs, yet it was a very great check to their industry and proceedings in their labour with that chearfulness they otherwise would have done. And what greatly contributed to their discontent was that one of the principle magistrates [Causton] hade the intire disposall and direction of the publick stores. By which all centered in him as having it in his power to starve the people into a compliance with his will and keeping from them the provissions alloted for them, if they in the least seem'd to disaprove or grumble at any measures he was disposed to take, but as there will be occassion to mention this hereafter in the memorialls I delivered to the Trustees, I shall proceed to consider the probability of succeeding in this new Colony, under the present Constitution and forme of Governmt. and offer such reasons as I humbly conceive will be an enternall barr to the undertaking as long as the law's and regulations of the Colony continue in the same shape they are in at present.

The success of all Colony's must depend upon the industry of its inhabitants, in cultivating and improveing the lands that are alloted to them, in order to produce (in the first place) provissions for their own subsistance, and in the next place some comodities for exportation to forreign markets, without which no Colony can long subsist, tho ever so powerfully supported. In order therefor to encourage the people to answear this great end, it is absolutely necessary not to cramp or oppress their minds with any harsh laws, and particularly not to clogg their right of inheritance to the fruits of their labour and industry, with harder terms and more forfeitures thane their fellow subjects in the neighbouring Colonys are lyable to. And above all the greatest care should be hade to setle such a forme of government as is agreable to them, and corresponding with the laws of the country they have been brought up in. And the executive part of this governmt. should be putt in the hands of persons fitly qualifyed, and who are not only distinguished for their superior capacities, humanities, and courage, but they should likewise be such as are in good esteem amongst and agreable to the people. If suffitient care be taken in these points and upon which I may venture to say the whole success depends, there is not in the least doubt but things would succeed (tho slowly) not withstanding the many hardships and difficulties such undertakeings must unavoidably be attended with.

But if on the contrary they should fall short of any of those necesary incouragements and the people find that they are upon a worss footing thane in any of owr Colonys in America it intirely unbends their minds from pursueing the principle thing of clearing and setling their lands; and they become quite tired of their undertakeing and many except those who by their places and oppressing the people, have an opportunity of amassing wealth, are kept by mere force wanting nothing but an opportunity of leaving the Colony and setling in some of the neighbouring provinces, which I know to be the case of many of the better sort of people as well as of the others, and who are only prevented from doeing it, by haveing exhausted the subsistance they brought with them, and necesarly oblidged to contract debts, which they are not in a condition of paying, and which is always found to be a suffitient reason for detaining them in the Colony.

But to proceed to the reasons which I apprehend will be a barr to the success of it I shall give but three, tho there are severall others which may not be so proper to be given. The first is the tenure by which the lands are held. The second is the prohibiting of negroes. And the third is the placing the governmt. in the hands of people who are so farr from being qualified or equall to so great a trust that they are looked upon with the greatest scorne and contempt by ever'y persone who has either seen or heard of their administration.

8. Land Tenure and Inheritance

As to the tenure of the lands the uncommon number of forfeitures contained in the grants, makes it almost impossible for any persone living to comply with them. And tho I am perswaded that no advantage would be taken if half the terms of the grants were not complyed with, yet the mere apprehension of it makes such an impression on the minds of the people that they must live in continuall fear of forfeiting their lands, knowing it almost impossible for them to comply with the conditions upon which they hold them. But this tho very discouraging is not near so fatall in its concequences as the setling the inheritance upon the male issue only and in failure of that to revert to the Trust, and thereby deprive daughters, brothers, and all other relations from enjoying what has been ever looked upon as a naturall right. This law is of its self alone suffitient to destroy the undertaking. For can any one imagine that a man who is posses'd of any property and who has that naturall tenderness and affection for his family and relations, which is common to mankind, would at the hazard of his own and their lives attended with a great expence and constant fatigue goe to setle in a countrey where if he chances to die without leaving a sone behind him, must have his lands with all the improvements he has made upon them, probably at a very considerable expense, revert to the Trust, and thereby leave his family, who hade been fellow labourers with him and shared in all his hardshipps so many sacrifises and unprovided for. Can one imagine I say that any man in his sences would goe to setle in any country upon those terms. The principle reasone that has been given for this law, is that by the inheritance descending in the male line, a suffitient number of men will be alwayes in the Colony to defend it in case of any attack, and that if the females should inherite, such a time might happen, when the whole Colony would be in the possession of women, and concequently defenceless and exposed a prey to any power who would invade her.

This reason how ever plausible it may appear at first has certainly no foundation in it, as has been suffitiently proved by instances, and can only be the child of some noted refiner of schemes. For supposing a man to die without male issue the Colony receives no emediate addition of strength by this, for that land would, must, doubtless be occupied by some persons already in the Colony or ly wast and neglected till the Trustee thought proper to dispose of it otherwise. And if they should think fitt to send people over from England to occupy that land, I cannot see how the Colony would receive any addition of strength even by that, because the Trustees have land enough in the Colony to give, without giving of that. Whereas on the contrary if the next of male kind or nearest male relation were to inherite (within a limited time) it would soon be occupied by some near relation, who would probably bring with him an additionall strength to the Colony, both of substance and people, which the Colony could never have received without such an accident, and in the mean time the relations who were upon the spott would make all the improvements they possibly could. This surely would be more agreable to justice and tend more to the advantage of the Colony thane to have the inheritance intirely cutt of [off] and the estates revert to the Trust, except the mansion house and one half of the inclosed lands, which the widdow's, in case there be any are intituled to the possession of, during their lives. But still the daughters would be in the same unhappy circumstances and cutt off from any hopes of inheriting or being provided for, upon a distant and most improbable supposition that a time might happen when the Colony would be wholly in the hands of women, and concequently defenceless.

European, and particularly English and other Brittish women, if they are sober and of good behaviour, are generally in good esteem and very valuable all over owr setlements both in the West Indies and in America, and it is seldome known that a woman of any merrite, lives long single in these countrys, but have the good fortune of being married, often to great advantage. Thane I think it will naturally follow that if the right of inheritance were in the daughters, in failure of male issue it would be a means rather of strengthning the Colony thane of weakning it, because the incouragement of having a setlement would certainly bring many young men not only from owr neighbour Colonys but like wise from other parts to marry those daughters and setle in the Colony, which would evidently prove to be a very great advantage to the Colony. And it would likewise be the means of increasing greatly the number of inhabitants and setlers and of making those who are already there more easy in their minds and more dilligent and industrious in their setlements. For I am perswaded that this law is one of the reasons why so small a progress has been yet made in the Colony, and has certainly prevented many people of subsistance from going to setle there.

9. *Negro Slaves and White Servants*

The second reasone is the prohibiting of negroes. I think it has hitherto been a received maxim in all owr southerne setlements, not only in the West Indies, but also in Carolina, that negroes are much more profitable to the planter (as being naturalisled to the extreame heats) thane any European servants whatsoever. And indeed daily experience showes that it is morrally impossible to doe without them, for it is to their labour joyned to their industry and good management of those who have hade the direction of them that owr Sugar Islands have made the great figure they have done, and to their labour is likewise owing the prodigious quantities of rice, which is yearly made in and exported from Carolina.

The reasons are very obvious: the first, because the climate is more naturall and agreable to them, and concequently they are less lyable to the distempers peculiar to hott country's by being daily exposed to the inclemency of the seasons. This is a truth so generally known that there needs nothing to be said to inforce it. The next reason is because they are much cheaper and more to be depended upon. For example, you purchass a new negroe, id est, a negroe just come from Guinea, for 20 pound sterling, which I take to be the midle price, given between the two extreams. This negroe we may suppose in the generall runn of negroes to be of a sound constitution and uncorrupted morralls, for it is certain that they are unaquainted with the many vices that are but too common amongst owr white servants, and almost in a state of inocency when compared to them and as he becomes your sole property, you may train him up in what manner you think will best answear your purpose, either to the field or to the house (which would not answear any end with a white servant, because his time is so short) and your negroe servant with good usage you may reasonably expect he will turne out a trusty and faithfull servant as long as he lives. For when ever it happens otherwise, it is too often owing to the barbarous cruelty their masters and overseers exercise over them, and I believe it has been observed by many people, as well as my self, that in proportion to the number of negroes and white servants, all over the West Indies and even in South Carolina the white servants generally turne out the worst. Nor can it be reasonably expected to be otherwise, because the common run of white servants that transport themselves to owr Colony's abroad by the help of owr agents for that purpose are generally the very scumm and refuse of mankind, trained up in all sorts of vice, often loaded with bad distempers and who leave their native country upon no other motive but to avoid the worss fate of being hanged in it. What can posibly be expected from such servants but that they would corrupt those you have before if they are not already as bad as themselves, for I am perswaded that of all the miserable objects on earth there is non make a worss figure thane the generall run of white servants abroad, owing intirely to their drunkeness and other vitious habits they hade contracted at home. On the contrary the negroes no where make a better appearance nor in the generall, doe I believe enjoy better health in their native country thane they doe in owr setlements.

The generall price of a common white servant, such as

has not been brought up to any particular trade, is ten or twelve pounds, for which sum you have him bound to you by indenture for the terme of four years, during which time you are to supply him with such cloathing as is suitable to the country and usually given in such cases, and he must also be supplyed with provisions which you must likewise doe to your negroe servants, but with this difference that your plantation negroes (who are the only negroes I would be understood to mean) as they are the most usefull negroes. For I look upon the great number of domestick negroes that are kept in the towns, generally for ostentation and grandeur (which is a custome but too prevailing all over owr settlements) to be both an impolitick and unprofitable one, but there is this difference between your white and negroe servants, that your negroes, having a small spott of land alloted to them, which is the common methode, doe by their industry and at their spare hours not only raise provissions suffitient for their own subsistance, but many of them raise poultry and other litle things, which by selling at market often enables them to buy great part of their own cloathing, so that the expence the master is at in supporting his negroes is but very small.

White servants must be treated in a quite different manner, for as they have from their infancy been accustomed to live in a different manner to what the negroes doe, so they must be fed and cloathed much better and concequently at a much greater expence; otherwise you cannot expect to receive any satisfaction or advantage from their servitude. So that I may venture to affirme that the difference of the expence in supporting a white and a negroe servant for the terme of four years (which is the time that white servants are generally bound for) will amount near if not fully to the difference of the prime cost of the negroe and the summ you pay for the white servant for four years. From which it appears even in this point that the negroe is so much cheaper to the planters thane the white servant, as the price the negroe will sell for at the end of four years, which at a moderate calculation may be reackoned at one third more thane the prime cost because negroes that have been trained up for that time either to plantation or any other bussiness, as they become more expert and better aquainted with the particular bussiness they are bred to, because concequently more valuable, and that advantage redounds solely to the propriator of the negroe.

And on the other hand, if a white servant should happen to proove well, the master can reap no further advantage from him, but during the time of his servitude. So that I think it is very apparant that negroes are not only much fitter thane white servants for hott climates, but they are likewise much cheaper and more beneficiall to the planter in ever'y respect. Nay it is morrally impossible that the people of Georgia can ever gett forward in their setlements or even be a degree above common slaves, without the help and assistance of negroes. Because the people of Carolina, who are remarkable for their industry and who inhabit a country equally as fine and productive as Georgia, will at all times, by the help of their negroes be able to undersell the people of Georgia in any commodities they can possibly raise, at any market in Europe. Which I think is suffitiently proved by the small progress, that is as yet made in Georgia. For it is plain to ever'y one who has been there that what is done has been done meerly by dint of money which would have been quite otherwise if the same number of negroes hade been imployed in that Colony as there has been of white people, they would have been able long before this time, not only to have subsisted themselves, but would likewise made a considerable figure in their exports, neither of which the people of Georgia are able to doe, nor can the wisest man living say when they will while the constitution of the Colony remains upon the same footing it does at present.

10. Opposition to the System of Government

The third reasone is the placing the Gouvernment of the Colonie in the hands of people that are not in any degree qualifyed for so great a trust as I hade the honour my self of being appoynted and continued First Bailiff for above two years (and till I apply'd to the Honble. the Trustees to have another appoynted in my room). I shall rather chuse to give some account of the magistrates and their gouvernment. From a letter wrote by a very worthy gentleman and friend, who was thane in Georgia, to his corrospondant in London, having obtained his leave for that purpose, and according as this shall be reviewed [I] shall be able to publish some other curious letters concerning the affairs of that Colony wrote by the same ingenious and other worthy friends. But at present shall content my self with giving you his sentiments of the magistrates and gouvernmt. rather thane speake my own, which I hope will be suffitient to show the evill concequences that attend a weak and disregarded gouvernment in an infant Colony.

Writing to his friend about some affairs relating to the Colony, he sayes, ["]Here is the cause that will confound us, the Chief Magistrate [Causton] we have here at present, who before he was advanced to this post and was only keeper of the publick stores, under the eye of Mr. Oglethorp, behaved himself in a modest civill manner and was really very dilligent and usefull in his place, is now so elated and puff'd up, his head so full of the dignity of his place and the honour and obedience the people are to pay him that in order to inforce this he runs into the most arbitrary and unjust proceedings, and those who doe not follow in with his measures, he procecutes with the utmost malice. Believe me what I say is not out of any personall pique, for his carriage to me has been very civill, and it is with reluctance that I make any complaint of him. But as the manifest good of the Colony requires it, I think it my duty. Nor shall I aledge any thing against him, but what I shall make evidently appear. If this humour of his amounted to no more thane what may be called a foible, a love of grandeur and ostentation, it would be excuseable, and whilst I apprehended it no worss I always discountenanced any complaints against him and advised all my friends to show him as much respect as he required, and thought it a stifness worthy of blame in them who could not bring their minds to it. And I shall not now alter my conduct in this respect, but whilst he continues in his post endeavour to make the people easy with him, tho I can't excuse him, as I have done because I have been my self a witness, together with the whole Court of a most flagrant piece of injustice, which I shall relate to you at large. But first must observe what a hardshipp the Colony is under, and those in particular who most stand in need of litle assistance and really deserves them, and yet cannot out of a principle of honesty or hon. [honour] come into his measures. These are sure to have his frowns whilst mean worthless fellows, who can fawn and flatter are his favourites.

["]With what justice may we expect such a one will discharge the litle trust repoze'd in him, of dealing out the provisions according to nesescity's and deserts of the people. This requires more discretion and impartiality thane he seems disposed to exercise. I call it trust repoze'd in him because the others who are joyned with him (excepting Mr. Gordon, who is now in England) viz. two more, as well in dispensing of justice as in the other affair. Yet he has so absolutely made himself master of them that they are to be considered no more thane cyphers. We live in hopes of having shortly one of the gentlemen of the Trust or some other gentleman of worth amongst us, to take the gouverment of the place upon him. The presence of such a one would be of vast service to us; nay I could almost say is absolutely necesary for upholding the Colony. There is a generall discontent with the present management, and I cannot say but very justly, for instead of an upright and faithfull dispensing of justice, instead of the magistrates being a terrour to evill doers and a praise to them that doe well.

["]Things are carried by prejudice and passion, by mean artifice and selfish designs of aquiring absolute power. Trick and cuning are universaly and deservedly esteem'd odious and detestable things in lessor matters, and why should they not appear much more so to honest and well designing men in maters of greater concequence in affairs of gouvernment and administration of justice, where the bad effects of them are more generall and lasting. Surely a persone must be farr gone in Machivilian principles to think them very criminall in one case and yet allowable and laudable in the other. It is certain that they can only serve the vile purposes of enslaving and destroying men, and I am sure the power that aims at those unworthy ends is not the power that is ordained of God.["]

You see here the sentiments of a very ingenious and worthy gentleman, which will be a great help in forming a right judgement of the gouverment of the Colony.

I shall now proceed to finish the journall during my stay in the Colony, for having by the hardshipps we underwent and living in a manner quite different from what I hade ever been accustomed to, contracted an illness which afterwards appear'd to be a fistula in ano, and owr surgeon Mr. Cox being dead, and no persone in the Colony from whome I could expect any relief, was oblidged to goe to Carolina, in order to gett the assistance of a surgeon there, who belong'd to Captain Massys Independent Company, where I continued three months during which time I was cutt three times and underwent incredible torture. But being informed by my surgeon that he hade compleated a cure, I returned to Savanah again, where in less thane a week I found my self so farr from being cured that I hade a returne of my illness worss thane ever, and there being litle hopes of meeting with a cure in that country I applyed to Mr. Oglethorp for leave to returne to England, which he granted, and wrote a letter along with me to George Heathcote Esq., one of the worthy Trustees recomending me to him and informing him in what manner I hade behaved my self.

And at the same time he assured me that by the next ship he would likewise write to the Trustees in generall in my behalf, which he could not at that time possibly doe, being so much hurryed in the affairs of the Colony that he hade scarce a moments time to spare, for at this time the Trustees hade not for some months heard from Mr. Oglethorp, nor know in what manner he was proceeding, so that he could not posssibly write to the Trustees on my account only, without giving them at the same time, an account of the situation of affairs in the Colony, which would have required more time thane he could possibly spare thene.

11. Gordon Returns to England

Nov: ye 4th [1733] Gouvernour Johnston,[37] Captain Massy, and Major Barnwell arrived at Savanah, to visit Mr. Oglethorp and the Colony, and the next morning Mr. Oglethorp ordered that the Corporation should waite upon the Gouvernour and the other gentlemen to welcome them to Savanah and to returne thanks to his Excellency for the favours he hade done to owr infant Colony, which we did and was received in a most obllidging manner. The same day his Excellency accompanied with Mr. Oglethorp and the other gentlemen sett out to visit Purisbourg and returned to Savanah the next day in their way to Charles Town.

November the eighth I sett out from Savanah, on my returne to England, and arrived at Charles Town the 12th and as soon as his Excellency, Gouvernour Johnston, to whome I brought letters from Mr. Oglethorp, heard of my arrivall, he with Captain Anson, who commanded one of His Majestys ships on that station, did me both honour of a visit at my lodgings, where they stayed above an hour and his Excellency invited me to dine with him the next day, which I did and during my stay received many civilitys from his Excellency and the gentlemen of Charles Town.

The 25th I sailed for England and arrived in London the 6th of January [1734]. As soon as I arrived, tho I was reduced to the weakest condition imaginable by my illness, yet before I putt my self under Mr. Chrisledons[38] care to be cutt for my fistula, I delivered all the letters and packets I was charg'd with and particularly that from Mr. Oglethorp to George Heathcote, Esq, who was extreamly glade to hear from Mr. Oglethorp and have an account of owr proceedings in the Colony. I hope this worthy gentleman will pardon me if now I cannot omitt mentioning with the utmost gratitude the severall very kind offers of assistance he was so good to make me in my ilness and [illegible] and severall marks of friendshipp I have since received from him and his family.

I also waited upon Mr. [James] Vernon, another of the worthy Trustees, who was also extreamly kind and very curious in inquiring into the state of the affairs of the Colony. As soon as I was in a condition of stirring abroad after Mr. Chrisledon hade cutt my fistula, I waited upon the Trustees at their office, and gave them the best account I was able, of the situation of affairs in the Colony, and at the same time presented to them a view of the new Town of Savanah, its situation, and manner it was laid out in, as likewise the forme and elevation of all the houses and other publick buildings that were compleated at the time I left it. The Trustees seem'd pleased with it, and order'd me to gett a compleat drawing made of it, which I presented to them as soon as it was finished, and for which they ordered me a small present.

As soon as Mr. Oglethorp arrived in England, he gave me an account of what additionall buildings hade been raised since my coming away, and desired that I would have it printed and dedicated to the Trustees, in which I was assisted by a subscription of many of the Honable. Trustees and other noblemen and ladies. The Indian Chiefs [39] who came over with Mr. Oglethorp, being soon to be sent home Mr. Oglethorp was very desirous that I should returne with them. Continued and confirmed in my office of First Bailiff, and at the same time and upon many other occassions, promised me his utmost friendshipp and assistance, I accordingly agreed to returne with the Indians, and applyed to Mr. Oglethorp, the affairs of the Colony being more emediately under his direction, for his instructions, in what manner I was to behave my self, in the execution of my office, looking upon my self not suffitiently qualified for the discharging an office of so great power without the assistance and particular directions of those I thought much better qualified thane my self. However, tho I frequently applyed for them yet I could never obtain any other thane not to oppose Mr. Causton in any steps he thought proper to take. This tho it gave me the greatest uneasiness, yet did not hinder me from persuing my resolution of returning.

12. Back in Georgia

And accordingly I imbarked at Gravesend on [a blank for the date, which was October 31] with the Indian Chiefs and about 50 Saltsburgers and as many English passengers, and arrived at Savanah in Georgia [a blank here for the date, which was December 27, 1734] where to my very great surprise I found the affairs of the Colony in the utmost confusion and so generall a dislike to the administration amongst the people, that many of them hade actually entered into one design before my arrival, of sending Mr. Causton, the principle magistrate, and against whom their complaints were chiefly grounded, home to England in irons. This design as soon as they heard of my arrivall they intirely laid aside in expectation that I was provided with full powers of redressing all their grievances, which from the knowledge they hade of me they assured themselves I would readily doe.

But not having received any particular instructions with regards to the execution of my office, tho I hade often applyed for them nor any power of inspecting into the publick stores, and seeing that justice was done to the poor people in the dispencing of them, which was one [of] the principle grievances complained of, I found that my power was not extencive enough effectually to relieve or redress them, tho it may be here objected that I being that

[End]

Notes

INTRODUCTION

1. For further information on this manuscript, see "Gordon's Manuscript," near the end of this Introduction.

2. Robert G. McPherson, ed., "The Voyage of the *Anne*—A Daily Record," in *Georgia Historical Quarterly*, XLIV (June, 1960), 227.

3. E. Merton Coulter, ed., "A List of the First Shipload of Georgia Settlers," *ibid.*, XXXI (December, 1947), 285; E. Merton Coulter and Albert B. Saye, eds., *A List of the Early Settlers of Georgia* (Athens: University of Georgia Press, 1949), 19.

4. For instances, see Thomas Causton, Savannah, March 12, 1732/33, to his wife, in Egmont Papers of the Phillipps Collection (in University of Georgia Library), No. 14200, p. 53; William Kilbury, Yamacraw Bluff (Savannah), February 6, 1732/33, *ibid.*, 29.

5. "The Minutes of the Common Council of the Trustees for Establishing the Colony of Georgia in America," being Volume II of Allen D. Candler, comp., *The Colonial Records of the State of Georgia* (26 volumes, less volume 20 which was never published. Atlanta: The Franklin Printing and Publishing Company, 1904-1916), II (1904), 11.

6. *South Carolina Gazette*, August 18 to 25, 1733.

7. Historical Manuscripts Commission, Manuscripts of the Earl of Egmont, *Diary of the First Earl of Egmont (Viscount Percival)* (3 volumes. London: His Majesty's Stationery Office, 1920, 1923), II (1923), 36-37; Robert G. McPherson, ed., *The Journal of the Earl of Egmont. Abstract of the Trustees Proceedings for Establishing the Colony of Georgia, 1732-1738* (Wormsloe Foundation Publications, Number Five. Athens: University of Georgia Press, 1962), 44.

8. Noble Jones to Trustees, July 6, 1735, in MS Colonial Records of Georgia (typescript on microfilm in University of Georgia Library), 203. See also *Egmont Diary*, II, 36; Candler, comp., *Colonial Records of Georgia*, II, 35-36 ff., 65.

9. What appears to be an original reprint of the Gordon engraving is in the De Renne Collection in the University of Georgia Library.

10. A copy of this plan is in the De Renne Collection in the University of Georgia Library.

11. George Dunbar to the Trustees, November 5, 1734, in MS Colonial Records of Georgia, XX, 11. See also Candler, comp., *Colonial Records of Georgia*, II, 72; McPherson, ed., *Journal of the Earl of Egmont*, 66; MS Colonial Records of Georgia (typescript on microfilm in University of Georgia Library), XXIX, 69.

12. Coulter and Saye, eds., *List of the Early Settlers of Georgia*, 101.

13. *Ibid.*

14. For an extended account of Watson, see Sarah B. Gober Temple and

Kenneth Coleman, *Georgia Journeys* (Athens: University of Georgia Press, 1961), 82–88.

15. Thomas Causton, Savannah, March 24, 1734/35, to the Trustees, in MS Colonial Records of Georgia, XX, 546.

16. *Ibid.*, 554.

17. James Ross McCain, *Georgia as a Proprietary Province. The Execution of a Trust* (Boston: Richard G. Badger, 1917), 209–12.

18. Elisha Dobree, Savannah, January 15, 1735, to the Trustees, in MS Colonial Records of Georgia, XX, 107.

19. Elisha Dobree, Savannah, January 27, 1735, to the Trustees, *ibid.*, 176.

20. Thomas Causton, Savannah, April 2, 1735, to the Trustees, *ibid.*, 576–77. Peter Gordon is listed as a Malcontent in a volume supposedly written by Thomas Stephens, one of the Malcontents, entitled *A Brief Account of the Causes That have retarded the Progress of the Colony of Georgia, In America; Attested upon Oath. Being a proper Contrast to the State of the Province of Georgia. Attested upon Oath; And some other Misrepresentations on the same Subject* (London, 1743), 95.

21. Candler, comp., *Colonial Records of Georgia*, II, 102.

22. Patrick Houstoun, Savannah, March 1, 1735, to Peter Gordon, in MS Colonial Records of Georgia, XX, 592–600.

23. Susan Bowling, Charles Town, March 20, 1735, to Peter Gordon, *ibid.*, 335–37.

24. Robert Parker, Sr., Savannah, March 2, 1735, to Peter Gordon, *ibid.*, 332–34. See also Patrick Houstoun, Savannah, January 21, 1735, to Peter Gordon, *ibid.*, 494–96; S. Quincy, Savannah, March 3, 1735, to Peter Gordon, *ibid.*, 600–603.

25. John West, Savannah, March 10, 1735, to Peter Gordon, *ibid.*, 605–606.

26. Joseph Watson, Savannah, March 10, 1735, to Peter Gordon, Charles Town, *ibid.*, 603–605.

27. Patrick Houstoun, Savannah, March 1, 1735, to Peter Gordon, *ibid.*, 592–600.

28. Thomas Christie, Savannah, March 19, 1735, to the Trustees, *ibid.*, 626.

29. Clarence L. Ver Steeg, ed., *A True and Historical Narrative of the Colony of Georgia, By Pat. Tailfer and Others with Comments by the Earl of Egmont* (Wormsloe Foundation Publications, Number Four. Athens: University of Georgia Press, 1960), 54, 55.

30. Peter Gordon, London, May 7, 1735, to the Trustees, in MS Colonial Records of Georgia, XX, 489–94.

31. *Egmont Diary*, II, 169.

32. Candler, comp., *Colonial Records of Georgia*, II, 102. See also McPherson, ed., *Journal of the Earl of Egmont*, 85; *Egmont Diary*, II, 174; Herman Verelst, Georgia Office (London), May 15, 1735, to Thomas Causton, Savannah, in MS Georgia Colonial Records, XXIX, 103–104.

33. *Egmont Diary*, II, 187; Thomas Causton, Savannah, July 25, 1735, to the Trustees, in MS Colonial Records of Georgia, XX, 226.

34. Herman Verelst, London, July 18, 1735, to Thomas Causton, Savannah, in MS Colonial Records of Georgia, XXIX, 142–43.

35. *Egmont Diary*, II, 191; McPherson, ed., *Journal of the Earl of Egmont*, 101–102.

36. *Egmont Diary*, II, 194; Candler, comp., *Colonial Records of Georgia*, II, 31 f., 120.

37. "Journal of the Trustees for Establishing the Colony of Georgia in

THE JOURNAL OF PETER GORDON 71

America," in Candler, comp., *Colonial Records of Georgia,* I (1904), 236.

38. Ver Steeg, ed., *True and Historical Narrative,* 54, 55.

39. *Ibid.*

40. Egmont made a slip in writing that Gordon "quitted" Georgia, April 12, 1738. See Coulter and Saye, eds., *List of the Early Settlers of Georgia,* 19.

41. *Egmont Diary,* II, 417; McPherson, ed., *Journal of the Earl of Egmont,* 286–87.

42. Candler, comp., *Colonial Records of Georgia,* II, 209; McPherson, ed., *Journal of the Earl of Egmont,* 310.

43. Candler, comp., *Colonial Records of Georgia,* II, 229. See also, "Original Papers, Correspondence, Trustees, General Oglethorpe and Others," in Candler, comp., *Colonial Records of Georgia,* XXI (1910), 468, 469; Herman Verelst, May 19, 1738, to Thomas Causton, in MS Colonial Records of Georgia, XXIX, 529–30; *Egmont Diary,* II, 478; McPherson, ed., *Journal of the Earl of Egmont,* 345.

44. Coulter and Saye, eds., *List of the Early Settlers of Georgia,* 69.

45. *Ibid.,* 19.

46. After this paragraph had been set in type, Mr. John Wyatt Bonner, Special Collections Librarian at the University of Georgia, found in the Keith Read Collection an intriguingly interesting letter relative to the Peter Gordon journal, from Anne Allison of New York, N. Y., to Keith Read, dated July 19, 1934. Efforts have been made without success to determine whether Anne Allison was a book dealer or an agent for one, or in what way she came into possession of the Gordon journal; but this letter does seem to establish the fact that Read secured it in 1934.

The pertinent part of the letter follows: "I am sorry you wouldn't ever come to see me so I could tell you about P. G. [Peter Gordon]—and with your unconquerable aversion to detail there's no use my writing you all the interesting things I've established after a large number of days at the library and fascinating hours digging through Georgia source material. However this much perhaps you will note— So far as I've been able to check up—all possibilities not yet exhausted but the major and important ones have been— Peter Gordon's journal has never been published and for the very good reason that the Trustees like N. R. A. [National Recovery Administration of the Franklin D. Roosevelt era] just weren't having any criticism. In addition to its being unpublished it is really an exceptionally interesting piece beyond its connection with Georgia beginnings and it is probably more valuable than the rest of your entire collection. Incidentally I was so impressed with its probable potential value after I had begun to check up on it that I have been keeping it in the vault of the bank." She notes that she is sending the journal to Read from Washington where she was stopping over for a week on her trip to Chicago, where she would be indefinitely.

THE JOURNAL OF PETER GORDON

1. This reference is to *Some Account of the Designs of the Trustees for Establishing the Colony of Georgia in America* (London, 1732?). This is a brief account in four pages, with a map of southern North America at the end.

2. The full title is *Reasons for Establishing the Colony of Georgia, with Regard to the Trade of Great Britain, the Increase of our People, and the Employment and Support it will Afford to Great Numbers of our Poor, as well as Foreign Persecuted Protestants. With Some Account of the Country,*

and the Design of the Trustees (London: W. Meadows, 1733). This booklet contains 48 numbered pages and ends with a repetition of the map which appeared in the *Designs*, listed in note 1, above.

3. Jean Pierre Purry, a Swiss colonial promoter, sought to induce the Georgia Trustees to give him permission to plant a settlement in Georgia. Some years before the Georgia project had been conceived of, he had written a pamphlet in 1724, which Gordon here alludes to, under the title of *Memorial Presented to his Grace the Duke of Newcastle* (London, 1724), describing the Carolina country and urging the English to push their settlements southward and westward. The Trustees refused Purry's request, and he then got permission from the South Carolina authorities to make a settlement on the Carolina side of the Savannah River a few miles above Savannah. This place became known as Purrysburg.

4. An account that might be considered official gives the total number of passengers as 114, instead of 96 as Gordon has it. See Coulter, ed., "List of First Shipload of Georgia Settlers," 282–88.

5. There are several biographies of James Edward Oglethorpe. The standard and most recent one is Amos Aschbach Ettinger, *James Edward Oglethorpe, Imperial Idealist* (Oxford, England: The Clarendon Press, 1936).

6. Henry Herbert, who falling ill in Georgia, died at sea on his return to England, June 15, 1733.

7. John Warren (Warrin) was a flax dresser by trade. He died in Savannah, August 11, 1733.

8. Samuel Parker died in Savannah, July 20, 1733.

9. Joseph Fitzwalter became a man of some importance in Georgia. In 1735 he married an Indian girl, who ran away from him. Later he married Penelope Wright, a widow. Fitzwalter was a gardener and was in charge of the Trustees Garden at Savannah several times. He died on October 28, 1742.

10. Richard Hodges was appointed a Conservator of the Peace and also, provisionally, a Bailiff, but he never served in the latter office. He died in Savannah, July 20, 1733.

11. Joseph Hughes was for a time the keeper of the Trustees Store. He died on September 30, 1733.

12. Richard Cannon died in Savannah, May 27, 1735.

13. William Kilberry's name does not appear in the list of passengers on the *Ann*, referred to in footnote 2, above; but he is included in another list as having arrived in Georgia, February 1, 1732–33, which list is in part the basis for Coulter and Saye, eds., *List of the Early Settlers of Georgia*, 81. Gordon's listing him as being on the ship seems to be definite proof of his presence; and the fact that he came to Georgia at his own expense may account for the fact that he did not appear on the list referred to in footnote 2, however illogical that may be. In compiling that list, the Earl of Egmont may purposely or by accident have omitted his name. It would, therefore, seem that there were 115 passengers instead of 114 in that first embarkation.

14. Probably escritoire, a writing table.

15. Dr. William Cox was the first of the Georgia settlers to die—April 6, 1733. His loss was sorely felt by those needing medical attention, though Noble Jones, another passenger on the first embarkation, administered to the sick when he could spare time from his several official duties.

16. Anne Coles was the wife of Joseph Coles, who died in Savannah, March 4, 1735. Anne re-married.

17. Francis Scott was appointed provisionally a Bailiff, but he never served. He died in Savannah, January 2, 1734.

18. Paul Amatis was an Italian silk man and gardener, from the province of Piedemonte. Soon after landing at Yamacraw Bluff he was sent to Charles Town to cultivate the Trustees Garden there, which was to be a sort of feeder for a time to the main Trustees Garden which was developed at Savannah. Amatis was brought to Georgia for the principal purpose of establishing the silk business, but he considered himself to be the head of the Trustees Garden in Savannah, too, where he planted a great many mulberry trees. In this assumption he had a long and bitter quarrel with Joseph Fitzwalter, who claimed to be the director of the Savannah garden. Eventually the Trustees settled the quarrel by making Amatis the director. Later he became disgruntled with Savannah, and went to Charles Town, where he died in December, 1736.

19. There is some confusion as to whether or not Oglethorpe was on board the *Ann* in its voyage from Charles Town to Port Royal. According to the following two works Oglethorpe had gone ahead by land: Temple and Coleman, *Georgia Journeys*, 7 and Henry Bruce, *Life of General Oglethorpe* (New York: Dodd, Mead, and Company, 1890), 102; but Oglethorpe himself in a letter to the Trustees dated January 13, 1732/33, in a postscript which he added after having gone ashore in Charles Town, said "I am just going to return on board 2 of the Clock in the Morning." Egmont Papers of the Phillipps Collection, No. 14200, p. 7 (typescript). Although this statement is anticipatory, there is no reason to believe that he did not board the ship. The confusion probably arises from the fact that Oglethorpe did set out from Port Royal in company with some South Carolinians to go on to Georgia ahead of the settlers, in order to locate a spot for their first town. This discussion as to whether or not Oglethorpe was on board the *Ann* has been considered of importance, for if he were not on board, then Gordon's account of the pirate ship would be suspect, for he says that Oglethorpe ordered preparations for the attack. Ettinger's *Oglethorpe* does not go sufficiently into details to make a statement one way or the other.

20. There are various ways in spelling the name of this particular kind of water craft, which are more-or-less accepted; but Gordon adds a few more spellings, using whatever combination of letters which suited his fancy at the time, without ever arriving at an accepted spelling. Spellings which have acceptance are: piragua, pirogue, pettiagua, and pettiauger. Piragua was the Spanish word, derived from the Caribs and Arawak Indians of the West Indies. The French transformed it into pirogue; and others in the course of time added the other spellings given above. This craft was a canoe made by hollowing out the trunk of a tree, and in a larger size, a flatboat with two masts without a deck or with one at each end. This latter version was the craft generally used by the colonists in trading along the coast and between Savannah and Charles Town.

21. February 12, "Georgia Day." The calendar problem has been discussed in the Introduction.

22. John Musgrove, a South Carolina trader, who had married a half-breed Indian girl, who later called herself "Queen of the Creeks" and caused the Colony much trouble.

23. Tomochichi (generally so spelled) was a remarkable chief of the Yamacraw Indians, who became a great friend of the Georgians. For an extended account of his life, see Charles C. Jones, Jr., *Historical Sketch of Tomo-Chi-Chi, Mico of the Yamacraws* (Albany, N. Y.: Joel Munsell, 1868).

24. William Bull, a prominent South Carolinian, who helped Oglethorpe lay out the town of Savannah. The principal street was named for him.

25. Peter de St. Julien (or James?), Benjamin Whitaker, Col. Nathaniel Barnwell, and Richard Woodward were prominent South Carolinians.

26. Thomas Causton, a calico printer by trade, was successively third, second, and first Bailiff (a term for judge or magistrate). Also he became the keeper of the Trustees Store. From almost the first he was a stormy figure in the history of Savannah and was finally turned out of office in 1739. His store accounts were much mixed up, and he went to England in 1743 in an attempt to straighten them out. In a further effort to do so, he was ordered by the Trustees to return to Georgia. In 1745 on his voyage back he died of spotted fever.

27. Noble Jones was one of the most important men in colonial Georgia, holding at one time or another almost every office in the Colony, except the governorship. He died in 1775. For an extended sketch of his life, see E. Merton Coulter, *Wormsloe, Two Centuries of a Georgia Family* (Wormsloe Foundation Publication, Number One. Athens: University of Georgia Press, 1955), 1–107.

28. James Goddard, one of the principal carpenters in the first embarkation, died in Savannah in July, 1733.

29. Thomas Christie had a long and turbulent career in Georgia, holding in succession several offices, including Recorder and Bailiff. For details of his life in Georgia, see Temple and Coleman, *Georgia Journeys*, 145–60.

30. Richard (John) Cameron was a servant to Francis Scott. He soon absconded to South Carolina.

31. William Osborne (?), a South Carolina patroon and pilot.

32. Apparently a South Carolina trader.

33. Jonathan Bryan (1708–1788) was born in South Carolina. He met Oglethorpe at Beaufort, and with others, accompanied him to the site on Yamacraw Bluff, where the town of Savannah was founded. Although much interested in Georgia, he did not move there until 1750. He held important offices under the Crown when the King took over Georgia. In the events leading up to the Revolution and in that struggle he was an outstanding Patriot. Although he was 67 years old at the outbreak of war, he joined the army and was captured and imprisoned by the British. See "Brampton Plantation," in *Georgia Historical Quarterly*, XXVII (March, 1943), 28 ff.; Frank B. Screven, "The Georgia Bryans and Screvens, 1681–1861," *ibid.*, XL (December, 1956), 325 ff.

34. Samuel Quincy arrived in Georgia in July, 1733, and returned to England two years later. A troublemaker and an unsatisfactory minister, he was recalled by the Trustees.

35. Unidentified.

36. William Waterland presided as Second Bailiff at this first session, but was dismissed the next month for misbehaviour (probably drunkenness). In February, 1734 he left for South Carolina, where he set up as a schoolteacher.

37. Robert Johnson, governor of South Carolina, 1730–1735.

38. Chrisledon was an eminent English surgeon in London.

39. In May, 1734 Oglethorpe set out for England, taking with him Tomochichi, his wife, his wife's brother, his nephew, Hillispilli (the war chief of the Lower Creeks), several other chiefs, and their attendants. After a visit of four months they returned, except one who had died of the smallpox. See Jones, Jr., *Tomo-chi-chi*, 58–71.

Index

Allison, Anne, sends Gordon manuscript to Keith Read, 71 (n. 46)
Amatis (Amatiss), Paul, Italian silk man, passenger on *Ann*, 31; career in Georgia and death, 73 (n. 18)
Anderson, Captain, South Carolina trader, 42, 74 (n. 32)
Ann (Anne), brings first colonists to Georgia, 1-3; threatened by pirates, 2; reaches Yamacraw Bluff, 3; voyage across Atlantic, 28-31
Anson, Captain, commander of British warship, 64
Arawaks, Indians, mentioned, 73 (n. 20)

Bailiff, 4, 49
Barnwell, Col. Nathaniel, South Carolinian, visits Savannah, 38, 64
Beachy Head, on coast of England, 29
Beaufort (Beauford Town), S. C., visited by passengers of *Ann*, 33, 34; mentioned, 42
Beverly Point, England, passed by *Ann*, 29
Bonner, John Wyatt, Special Collections Librarian at University of Georgia, finds letter, 71 (n. 46)
Bryan (Brian), Jonathan, treats with Indians, 43; comes to Georgia, sketch of life, 74 (n. 33)
Bull, William, helps colonists, 37; treats with Indians, 42

Calendar, explanation of Old Style and New Style, 3
Cameron, Richard (John), servant, searches for jail breaker, 40; sketch, 74 (n. 30)
Cannon (Canon), Richard, passenger on *Ann*, 29; child dead, 29-30; dead, 72 (n. 12)
Captains Bluff, 48

Caribs, Indians, mentioned, 73 (n. 20)
Cattle, in Georgia, 42
Causton, Thomas, Bailiff, charges against, 9, 12, 13, 14, 16, 49, 60-61, 66; Tythingman, 38, short sketch, 74 (n. 26)
Charles Town, *Ann* anchors at, 2, 31; mentioned, 4, 13, 18, 37, 40, 41, 42, 46, 64
Chester Castle, mentioned, 21
Chisledon (Chisleden), London surgeon, attends Gordon, 5, 65, 74 (n. 38)
Christie, Thomas, Savannah resident, searches for jail breaker, 40; appointed Recorder, 49; sketch, 74 (n. 29)
Coles, Joseph, passenger on *Ann*, 31; death, 72 (n. 16)
Coles, Mrs. Joseph, passenger on *Ann*, 31, as widow, remarries, 72 (n. 16)
Colleton, John, South Carolinian, visits Georgia, 48-49
Colonies, settlement in ancient times, 23-24
Conservators of the Peace, in Georgia government, 4
Constables, in Georgia government, 4, 50
Cook, Ann, received Gordon property in Georgia, 17
Cook, Susannah, received Gordon property in Georgia, 17
Cook, William, daughters received Gordon property in Georgia, 17
Cox, Dr. William, surgeon, dead, 4, 45, 72 (n. 15); passenger on *Ann*, 30; in Georgia, 36

De Renne Collection, View of Savannah, 69 (ns. 9, 10)
Downs, on coast of England, 28-29
Dunbar, George, ship commander, 9

Earl of Egmont, comments on Joseph Watson, 10; comments on Gordon, 13–14; mistake on date of Gordon's leaving Georgia, 71 (n. 40); does not record William Kilberry on list of passengers on *Ann*, 72 (n. 13)

Farringtone, Lieutenant, soldier, 36
Fitzwalter, Joseph, passenger on *Ann*, 29; career in Georgia, 42, 72 (n. 9), 73 (n. 18)
Frenchman, jail breaker from Charles Town, 41

Georgia, founded, 3; civil government set up, 3–4; deaths, 4; early settlers unsuited for new life, 9–10; charter, 24–25; criticism of civil government, 49–53, 60–62; land tenure and inheritance, 53–56
Georgia Day, celebrated, 3
Goddard, James, Tythingman, 38; dead, 74 (n. 28)
Gordon, Catherine, wife of Peter, 2, 17
Gordon Manuscript, description of contents, 18–19; purpose, 19–20; when written, 20; course of ownership, 20–21, 71 (n. 46); method of its editing, 21–22; text, 23–67
Gordon, Peter, importance in England, 1; appointed Tythingman, 1, 30; sick on voyage, 2; asked by Oglethorpe to go ashore at Charles Town, 2; First Bailiff, 3, 49; Conservator of the Peace, 4; illness and trip to Charles Town, 4, 63; returns to England for treatment, 4–5, 63, 64; makes report on Georgia to Trustees, 5–6; presents View of Savannah to Trustees, 6; returns to Georgia, 8–9, 65–66; defends Joseph Watson, 11; condemns Thomas Causton, 12–13, 16; returns to England with complaints of colonists, 12–13; addresses letter to Trustees, 14–15; appears before Trustees, 15; presents letters of discontent and Memorial, 15–16; condemned by Trustees and dismissed as Bailiff, 16; remains in England and gives up property in Georgia, 17; death, 17–18; account of threat by pirates, 32–33, 73 (n. 19); condemns form of civil government in Georgia, 49–53, 60–62; condemns land tenure and inheritance in Georgia, 53–56
Gravesend, England, point of departure of Georgia colonists, 28, 66
Gray, Savannah resident, 46

Heathcote, George, Georgia Trustee, mentioned, 63, 64
Herbert, Henry, preacher, sermon to Georgia colonists, 29; baptizes child, 29; buries child at sea, 30; goes to Beaufort, 33; goes to Charles Town, 41; dead, 46, 72 (n. 6)
Hillispilli, Indian chief, visits England, 74 (n. 39)
Hodges, Richard, passenger on *Ann*, 29; career in Georgia and death, 72 (n. 10)
Houstoun, Patrick, Scotsman, agent for Gordon, 13
Hughes (Huges), Joseph, passenger on *Ann*, ill, 29; breaks toe, 30; owns servant, 40; appointed Registrar, 49; career and death, 72 (n. 11)

Indians, living near Savannah, 5; welcome colonists, 35–36; treat with Oglethorpe, 43–45, 48–49; visit England and return, 65–66, 74 (n. 39)
Inheritance, in Georgia, 53–56
Isle of Wight, passed by Georgia colonists, 29

Johnson, Robert, governor of South Carolina, entertains Gordon, 5; visits Savannah, 64; governorship of South Carolina, 1730–1735, p. 74 (n. 37)
Jones, Mr., minister at Beaufort, S. C., 34
Jones, Noble, helps the sick, 4, 72 (n. 15); remarks on Gordon's View of Savannah, 6–7; Tythingman, 38; short sketch, 74 (n. 27)
Jones's Island, on South Carolina coast, 34, 35

Keith Read Manuscript Collection, in University of Georgia Library, 21, 71 (n. 46)

INDEX

Kilberry (Kilbery), William, passenger on *Ann*, 30, 31; goes ashore at Port Royal, 33; in Georgia, 41; name not on Earl of Egmont's list of *Ann* passengers, 72 (n. 13)

Land tenure, in Georgia, 53–56
Lower Creeks, mentioned, 74 (n. 39)

Malcontents, oppose Trustees, 12; condemn Thomas Causton, 14, 15, 16–17
Massey (Massy), Philip, commander of Independent Company, 34, 42; visits Savannah, 64
Maxwell, P., owner of Gordon manuscript, 21
Middletone, Mr., pilot at Charles Town, 31
Musgrove (Musgrave), John, Indian trader, welcomes colonists, 35, 36, 37, 73 (n. 22); owns cowpens, 39; helps treat with Indians, 43
Musgrove, Mary, Indian woman, accused by Gordon, 12–13

New Style. *See* Calendar

Oglethorpe, James Edward, brings first colonists to Georgia, 1–3, 29, 30, 31, 32; lives in tent, 5, 37; asks Gordon to conduct Indians back to Georgia from visit to England, 8; landing at Yamacraw Bluff, 35; provides for a settlement on Tybee Island, 40; deals with Indians, 42, 43–45, 48–49; drives first nail in first house finished in Savannah, 42; takes Indians to visit in England, 74 (n. 39)
"Oglethorps Sub Sheriff," owner of Gordon manuscript, 21
Old Style. *See* Calendar
Osborne (Osbourne), William, a South Carolina patroon, 41, 74 (n. 31)

Parker, Samuel, passenger on *Ann*, 29; dead, 72 (n. 8)
Periagaes, water craft, described, 33, 73 (n. 20)
Pirates, threaten *Ann*, 2, 32, 33, 73 (n. 19)

Port Royal, S. C., *Ann* anchors at, 2, 31–32, 33; mentioned, 18
Prince of Wales, voyage to Georgia, 8–9
Privy Council, hears Watson case, 11
Purry, Jean Pierre, Swiss colonial promoter, 25, 33, 72 (n. 3); visits Georgia, 40–41
Purrysburg, South Carolina colonial settlement, 33, 40, 64, 72 (n. 3)

Quincy, Samuel, minister, arrives in Georgia, 46, 74 (n. 34)

Read, Keith, owner of Gordon manuscript, 21; estate sells manuscript to Wormsloe Foundation, 21; receives journal from Anne Allison, 71 (n. 46)
Recorder, in Georgia government, 4, 49, 50
Register, office in Georgia government, 49
Richardson, Richard, owner of Gordon manuscript, 21
Roman Colonies, 23

Salzburgers (Saltsburgers), come to Georgia, 66
Savannah, View, 1, 6; deaths, 4, 45; location, 5; landing of colonists, 35; fortifications, 37; fire breaks out, 37–38; conditions, 38–48; burial of the dead, 45–46; well dug, 46. *See also* Georgia
Scott, Francis, passenger on *Ann*, 31, 33, 34; career in Georgia, death, 35, 40, 41, 43, 46–48, 72 (n. 17)
Servants, white, in Georgia, 57–60
Silk business, 73 (n. 18)
Slaves, Negro, hired in Georgia from South Carolina, 43; Gordon favors, 56–57
Smith, Samuel, Georgia Trustee, sermon to Georgia colonists, 28
St. Augustine, Florida, mentioned, 43
St. Julien, Peter de (or James?), South Carolinian, visits Savannah, 38, 48–49

Thomas, Captain, commander of the *Ann*, 28, 31

Tomochichi (Tomo Chachi), Indian king, 8; welcomes colonists, 35–36, 37; friend of Georgians, 42, 73 (n. 23); visits England, 74 (n. 39)

Town Clerk. *See* Recorder

Trustees, Georgia, receive Gordon report, 5–6; condemn and dismiss Gordon as Bailiff, 16; establish colony of Georgia with terms of settlement, 25–28; policies condemned by Peter Gordon, 49–63

Trustees Garden, 72 (n. 9), 73 (n. 18)

Trustees Store, 72 (n. 11)

Tybee Island, on Georgia coast, mentioned, 40

Tybee Light, neglected, 14

Tythingmen, office in Georgia government, 50

Tythings, set up, 38

Uchees (Uchis), Indians, mentioned, 44, 48

University of Georgia Library, owns Peter Gordon manuscript, 1, 21

Upper Creeks, mentioned, 48

Verelst, Herman, writes friendly letter to Thomas Causton, 15–16

Vernon, James, Georgia Trustee, mentioned, 65

View of Savannah, sketch, 1, 6–8, 69 (ns. 9, 10)

Warren, Georgia Marino, child born on *Ann*, 29

Warren (Warrens, Warrin), John, father of son born on *Ann*, 29; in Georgia, 37; dead, 72 (n. 7)

Waterland, William, second Bailiff, 49; sketch, 74 (n. 36)

Watson, Joseph, troubles and indictment, 10–11

Whitaker, Benjamin, South Carolinian, visits Savannah, 38, 39, 42

Woodward, Richard, South Carolinian, visits Savannah, 38

Wormsloe Foundation, presents Gordon manuscript to University of Georgia Library, 21

Wright, Penelope, marries Joseph Fitzwalter, 72 (n. 9)

Yamacraw Bluff, mentioned, 3, 35

CPSIA information can be obtained
at www.ICGtesting.com
Printed in the USA
LVHW092031161021
700652LV00006B/188